W9-ADY-024

Crosscurrents / MODERN CRITIQUES

Harry T. Moore, *General Editor*

The French Parnassian Poets

Robert T. Denommé

WITH A PREFACE BY

Harry T. Moore

SOUTHERN ILLINOIS UNIVERSITY PRESS
Carbondale and Edwardsville

FEFFER & SIMONS, INC.
London and Amsterdam

To the memory of my Parents

Contents

Preface

Few countries in the nineteenth century had so vigorous an opposition to Romanticism as that provided by the Parnassians in France.

Romanticism had taken a strong hold there after the revolution at the end of the eighteenth century. Napoleon, for all the pictures and descriptions of him in columned buildings done in the Classical style, was essentially a Romantic. When he met Goethe, he told the author of Werther he had read that novel seven times, carrying it in his saddlebag on campaigns. Werther (1774) was one of the first influential Romantic books; between 1776 and 1779, it was translated fifteen times, and had almost as powerful effect on young Frenchmen as upon the youthful Germans who adopted the Werther costume.

English Romanticism also flourished in French translations, and Chateaubriand's Génie du Christianisme (1802) helped stimulate interest in English books. But the crest came in 1830, with the production of Hugo's Hernani, rumored to be too innovative and radical for conservative theatergoers to approve of. When on the opening night they tried to beat down the actors by shouting and clapping, the young Romanticists cheered the play on, as they were also to do at the second performance. Théophile Gautier, the painter who was to become a poet, was among the Romantics on those occasions, wearing the red jacket which was to become famous. In the present book, Professor Denommé of the University of Virginia shows how Gautier, as a poet, left the Romantics and went on into the Art for Art's Sake movement as well as a forerunner of the group which called itself the Parnassians, taking the name from that of the books of new poetry issued as Le Parnasse contemporain.

The leading poets of the new movement, which subscribed to the anti-Romantic disciplines outlined by, Gautier, were Théodore de Banville, Charles-Marie-René Leconte de Lisle, and José-Maria de Herdia, with each of whom Professor Denommé deals at length, following his introductory discussion of the entire Parnassian movement and his analysis of Gautier's career as a poet. Mr. Denommé translates various poems by these four men, with his own prose translations, and he provides a valuable survey of all this material, never becoming too technical but always presenting useful insights.

Professor Denommé, the author of an earlier Cross-currents book, The Nineteenth-Century French Romantic Poets, here takes up the cause of the Parnassians, who have been too-long neglected. He has given us just the right book for a fuller understanding of some French poets who deserve to become better known.

HARRY T. MOORE

Southern Illinois University
February 17, 1972

Introduction

A significant number of critics and historians of recent vintage have been content to relegate French Parnassianism to the more remote and obscure corners of nineteenth-century literature. The following essays are a study of the theory and practice of the poetry of its leading exponents. A conscious attempt has been made to situate the Parnassian lyric within the larger context of the positivist, "scientist," and realist currents which left an important impression in the French mind during the Second Empire. The first chapter, "From Art for Art's Sake to Parnassianism," surveys the evolution of poetic expression from the ebullience of social Romanticism in the 1830s and 1840s to the rise of Symbolism in the 1880s and 1890s. The subsequent essays on the verse of Théophile Gautier, Théodore de Banville, Leconte de Lisle, and José-Maria de Heredia serve as illustrations of the predominant theories and attitudes of Parnassianism.

To make this study accessible to the general reader as well as to students in French and Comparative literature, I have kept the purely technical considerations on French versification to an essential minimum. I have translated into English the passages that are quoted to substantiate various points that are made. Prose approximations follow the verse that is cited, and all but the most obvious titles have been rendered into English at least once.

I wish to express my deep appreciation and indebtedness for the reading of the entire manuscript by the late Professor Joseph-M. Carrière.

ROBERT T. DENOMMÉ

Charlottesville, Virginia
November 15, 1971

1

From Art for Art's Sake to Parnassianism

As significant literary currents of the nineteenth century, Art for Art's Sake and Parnassianism rose in open reaction to the types of social and utilitarian Romanticism that came to dominate the two decades of the July Monarchy. Just as the earliest Romanticists sought the freedom of literary expression from the constraint and rigidity of lingering neoclassical formulas during the years immediately following the French Revolution, the most forceful exponents of Art for Art's Sake and Parnassianism advocated the liberation of art from the kind of didacticism that tended to render it subservient to specific causes and programs during the reigns of Louis-Philippe and Louis-Napoleon from 1830 to 1870.

Despite a mutually articulated goal of autonomy in literature and other notable resemblances in attitude, Art for Art's Sake and Parnassianism underscored sufficiently distinguishing features that precluded their assimilation into any single prevailing literary movement. In their reaction to lyrical expression during the 1830s and 1840s, the leading proponents of Art for Art's Sake attempted a redefinition of Romanticism by suggesting a change of emphasis from the highly imaginative recreation of ideal truth to the more accurate observation and objective reproduction of concrete reality. It is no exaggeration to say that Art for Art's Sake pleaded for considerably more than the expurgation of all forms of partisanship from literature; it encouraged the supplantation of the emotional and sentimental appeal in lyricism by a more disciplined aesthetic preoccupation.

The leading advocates of Parnassianism staunchly upheld the main tenets of the practitioners of Art for Art's Sake, in large measure, because they concurred with their own ambitious designs for the reform and renewal of the rhetoric of the French lyric. Doubtless impressed by some of the positivist currents dominating the 1850s and 1860s, the most prominent Parnassian poets supported an alliance with scientific methodology in order that the observation of external reality might be achieved with the calm deliberation of the scholar rather than with the enervating passion of the unpredictable lyricist. Whatever differences of opinion and interpretation may have ultimately separated the proponents of Art for Art's Sake from their congeners in Parnassianism, these two literary attitudes contributed significantly to the transformation of French Romanticism from a philosophical conception of life to a considerably more genuine literary doctrine.

To a large degree, the reforms of Art for Art's Sake and Parnassianism managed to counterbalance the mysterious inner reality which preoccupied Romanticism with the more critical appreciation of external reality which concerned such distinguished poets as Théophile Gautier and Leconte de Lisle.

It would be erroneous to assume that the growing encroachment of industry, economics, and politics upon Romantic literature passed unnoticed or went uncriticized until the publication of Gautier's celebrated manifesto on Art for Art's Sake in the preface to *Albertus* in 1832. Such divergent public personalities as the socialist thinker, Proudhon, and the literary critic, Sainte-Beuve, warned of the degeneracy of literary expression through the increasing collaboration between art and commerce.[1] Along with such lesser-known figures as Gustave Planche and Saint-René Taillandier, literary and social commentators during the opening years of the July Monarchy, Sainte-Beuve voiced his dismay over the casual manner in which increasing numbers of writers had so blatantly compromised their talents to satisfy and flatter the questionable artistic trends of a rapidly expanding industrialized bourgeoisie. To complicate matters, such notable ideological groups as the Saint-Simonians and the Fourierists, to mention but the most prominent, vigorously enlisted the aid of writers to further the cause of the transformation of France into a highly contrived social and political utopia.

The overwhelming majority of writers in the 1830s and 1840s either endorsed and campaigned tirelessly in behalf of the various ideological aspirations of what became known as social Romanticism or quietly consented to the practice of popular literature for the sake of swift personal recognition and financial gain. As early as 1830, it had grown increasingly evident that both the social Romanticists and the so-called industrial artists had placed the autonomy of "pure" literature in serious jeopardy.

When Gautier's dramatic plea for Art for Art's Sake appeared in 1832, it was contemptuously dismissed as the ranting supplication of a bohemian whose irresponsibility prevented him from adjusting his poetic vision to the pragmatic sights of a regime conspicuously confident of the nature of its social mission. Gautier's critics in 1832 curiously echoed the characteristic objection of Charles de Rémusat in the *Globe* of 1825: "Man was not created so that he might merely sing, believe, and love without any specific purpose or objective." [2] Gautier's preface to *Albertus* nevertheless constituted the first significant thrust in defense of *le romantisme artiste* at precisely the moment when most cultural programs were undergoing drastic pragmatic revisions under the impulse of the Industrial Revolution.

The theory of Art for Art's Sake, as Théophile Gautier understood it in 1832, rested upon a conception of ideal beauty rooted at least partially in attitudes projected at various intervals by such eighteenth-century German aestheticians as Kant, Hegel, and Schiller. All advocated, with deliberate forcefulness, a philosophy of art which underscored complete independence from any moral, social, or scientific consideration. Their respective ideas on the idealization of beauty, based largely upon imaginative and abstract interpretations of reality, made their way into France at least casually if not systematically in the treatises and lectures of such critics of French Romanticism as Madame de Staël, Victor Cousin, and Théodore Jouffroy.

Specific reference to the theory of ideal beauty appeared as early as 1813 in Book Two of Madame de Staël's *De l'Allemagne* [Concerning Germany] where credit is ascribed to the German archaeologist, Wincklemann, for having developed the principles of idealization in the arts as residing in the imagination rather than outside the mind of the artist.[3] In a subsequent allusion to the theory of ideal beauty, Madame de Staël translates her familiarity with the Kantian doctrine on the independence of art and comments: "The Germans do not consider, as we ordinarily do, that the imitation of nature constitutes the primary objective of art; it is the idealization of beauty which appears to them to be at the root of all literary and artistic masterpieces." [4]

Shortly after his return from Germany in 1817, Victor Cousin endorsed the Kantian distinction on the autonomy of art and elaborated upon Wincklemann's conception of ideal beauty in a protracted series of lectures in 1818 which were subsequently published in book form as *Du Vrai, du beau et du bien* [Concerning truth, beauty, and morality] in 1836. Much of the thrust behind Cousin's hypothesis on the nature of ideal beauty constituted hardly more than a well-presented paraphrase of Quatremère de Quincy's *Essais sur l'idéal* [Essays concerning idealism] which came under heated academic debate and discussion in 1805.[5] In the seventh lesson of his treatise, for example, Cousin summarizes the major theses of Wincklemann and de Quincy when he points out that the essence of beauty does not reside in the artful imitation of nature, and that the object of the artist's contemplation should be the ideal rather than the realist interpretation of nature in all of its contingencies.[6]

In a similar fashion, Théodore Jouffroy argued in 1825 that the concepts of beauty and utility represented a contradiction in terms, and that the very notion of art excluded all predetermined causes and objectives.[7] What is particularly noteworthy about the passages under discussion is their uniform defense of the function of the imagination in art and literature. The implicit and explicit rejection of the principle of utility by Madame de Staël, Victor Cousin, and Théodore Jouffroy would win the predictable endorsement of both the proponents of Art for Art's Sake and Parnassianism, but the importance ascribed to the role of the imagination would only gain the cautious approval of such practitioners of Art for Art as Théophile Gautier and the gentle yet firm admonition of the more scientifically oriented Parnassians as Leconte de Lisle.

Even the most casual examination of the early theoretical pronouncements of prominent exponents of social Romanticism discloses some startling resemblances in disposition with what will become known as Art for Art's Sake or literary bohemianism after 1832. Consideration of Victor Hugo's wavering attitude between noncommitment and commitment in literature during the 1820s and 1830s, for example, brings into sharper perspective the nature of the ideological principles which divided the advocates of the two literary stances in question. In his several pleas in behalf of the priorities of literary expression over the inhibition of rigid classical formulas, Hugo came astonishingly close to proclaiming the gratuity of art.

The 1826 preface[8] to *Odes et Ballades*, which argued against the lack of any apparent aesthetic justification for the classical rule on the separation of the *genres*, brought Hugo closer to the position of Théophile Gautier. The preface to the *Orientales* in 1829 brought him virtually to the brink of declaring complete autonomy for the poet, and provoked the obvious displeasure of Pierre Leroux and Hippolyte Carnot, the cofounders of the *Revue encyclopédique,* who admonished Hugo for advocating and writing verse of little or no consequence with relation to the predicaments of modern man.[9] Hugo's flirtation with Art for Art's Sake reached its apogee in 1830, ironically at the very moment when French Romanticism scored its first major victory over the lingering yet stubborn supporters of neoclassicism. *Hernani* accomplishes significantly more than project the portrait of a fatalistic individual; the drama asserts the notion of a gratuitous freedom with the kind of boldness rarely encountered before in French literature. When Hugo's protagonist, Hernani, declares to Doña Sol "I am propelled by a force that goes," the dramatist proclaims through the admission of his character that poetic freedom excludes any commitment to a preconceived or predetermined cause. It remains a fact that the poetic hero of Hugo's drama remains conspicuously faithful to the uninhibited impulses of his own imagination by rejecting all forms of temporary or practical relationships.

Such potential disciples as Alfred de Musset and Théophile Gautier were quick to register their disappointment in the discernible shift in tone and mood of Hugo's literary conception after 1830. The change of emphasis in the poet's attitude may be detected in the publication of a curious preface which Hugo was prompted to write after an official ban had been placed on his drama, *Le Roi s'amuse* [The king is enjoying himself], in November of 1832 by the July Monarchy, ostensibly on the grounds of immorality. The essay is naturally divisible in two parts because of the unexpected turn of the polemical arguments half way through the preface.

The treatise begins, predictably, with a virulent at-

tack on the spirit of repression that ordered the play
banned, and by the poet's solemn resolve to struggle in
behalf of the establishment of freedom of expression in
the theatre. The fact of the matter was that the opening arguments in favor of a liberated theatre gave
familiar indications of disintegrating into a sequel to
the *Préface à Cromwell* [Preface to Cromwell] of 1829.
The sudden jolt in Hugo's plea occurs when he openly
questions his attitude of detachment from political,
social, and moral considerations in literature. The tenor
of the rest of the essay is one of acquiescence and resignation: "The poet has his own task to perform; he
knows what he must do, and nothing must deter him
from fulfilling his obligation. At the moment, he has
acquired a political responsibility which he did not seek
but which he accepts willingly." It is no small irony that
Hugo's admittedly reluctant subversion of art to political designs occurred at precisely the moment when he
meant to protest the political interference which resulted in the ban placed on *Le Roi s'amuse.*

If it is true that 1832 marked the beginnings of
Hugo's allegiance to the conception of a utilitarian
literature, the same year also signaled the start of
Théophile Gautier's almost relentless campaign in behalf of an aesthetics of Art for Art's Sake in France.
After the July Revolution of 1830, the Saint-Simonians
and the Fourierists had succeeded in luring the majority
of the leading Romanticists from their respective
cénacles and drawing rooms into the public arena of
political and ideological activism. The preface to
Albertus pointed to the literary crossroads at which
Victor Hugo and Théophile Gautier had arrived. Gautier's prefatory treatise constitutes a rather convincing
argument for autonomy in art, and issues a scathing
denunciation of the degrading compromises to which
the social Romanticists had subjected literature with
their propaganda:

What cause does art serve? It serves the cause of
beauty. Isn't that enough? Like the flowers, like per-

fume, like the birds, like all that man has been unable to deprave and subvert to meet his own
ends. . . .

. . . Art is freedom, luxury, efflorescence; it's the
blossoming of the soul in idleness. Painting, sculpture, music serve no purpose whatsoever, yet who
would dare think of doing away with them? [10]

The advocacy of the independence and gratuity of art
and literature is made to rest on a principle which
Gautier reveals with quasi-aphoristic force: "Generally,
when something becomes useful, it ceases to be
beautiful." [11]

The 1835 preface to *Mademoiselle de Maupin* reinforced with still more vehemence the thesis on the
autonomy of art advanced some three years earlier in
the introductory essay to *Albertus*. Both the preface to
Mademoiselle de Maupin and the novel itself unveil in
particularly revealing terms the nature of the aesthetic
code devised by Gautier and the reason that motivated
its adoption. The prefatory essay translates with sharp
humor and characteristic vividness his belief that art is
not a generative force for what may be considered good
or useful but that it is solely an instrument of beauty.
Listen to his categorical dismissal of utilitarianism in
art: "Only that which cannot serve a purpose may be
considered truly beautiful. Everything that is useful is
ugly, for usefulness expresses human needs, and they are
base and debilitating. The most useful rooms in a house
are the latrines." [12]

The fiction itself appends the conception of plasticity
to the notion of autonomy in art and tends to equate it
with the manifestation of ideal beauty. To a significant
degree, Gautier embodies the aesthetic stance of his
protagonist, D'Albert, whose sensory and emotional
satisfaction are gratified through the contemplation of
idealized beauty. For Gautier and D'Albert, an identification is made between the conception of beauty and
the visual forms that are emphasized by the artist:
"Three things please me: gold, marble and the crimson

dyes of the Ancients: flashes of light, solidity of form, color. My dreams are made of such stuff, and all the castles of my dreams are constructed with these materials." [13] The importance ascribed to the concrete and plastic interpretations of art in *Mademoiselle de Maupin* were destined to receive fuller elaboration in the collection of poems Gautier published in 1852 and 1857, *Emaux et Camées* [Enamels and Cameos].

The probable explanation of Gautier's complete rejection of the more personal aspects of Romanticism during the mid-1830s may be found in the frenetically fanciful effusions of his first poems, collected and published in 1830. His early poetry betrays a near-obsessive concern with the ephemeral and fragile nature of human life. The personal distress he experienced through the more metaphysical interpretations of existence infused him with a sense of inadequacy and dejection which he attempted with dogged determination to dispel.

The great chasm that existed between human aspiration and limited achievement, and his intense consciousness of life's transitoriness eventually induced him to retreat behind a mask of impassibility before the urgent immediacies of everyday situations in order to gain a measure of the mental tranquility which he urgently sought. Gautier elected to withdraw from the immediacy of the contingencies of daily existence and learned to stifle or control his own emotions and reactions so that he might avoid the expenditure of energy upon matters of little or dated significance. To achieve his aim, he steeped himself in the conception of hellenic serenity which permeated the bucolic verse of André Chénier.

He eventually evolved the kind of poetic disposition which, although somewhat inclined toward immobility, would allow him to obtain at least the quiet illusion of permanence from a world bereft of such values. The fact of the matter was that Gautier's aesthetic attitude, stripped of all utilitarian concern, corresponded to his deep-seated interest in painting and the plastic arts since it emphasized the sensory reproduction and idealization of reality. In his search for ideal beauty through the observation of external nature, he concluded that the work of art constituted the only lasting value in an otherwise overwhelmingly valueless world. Through the creation of works of lasting beauty, the artist could convince himself of the continuity and the perpetuation of human aspirations that somehow rendered his otherwise heterogeneous view of man's predicament considerably more homogeneous.

The contemplation of the artistic legacy bequeathed modern man by the ancient epochs and civilizations provided Gautier with the most ideal means by which he could achieve the type of remoteness from the pragmatic concerns of the contemporary situation that his new aesthetic code required. The artistic expression of Greek Antiquity, for example, afforded him the splendid opportunity of viewing its masterpieces with the kind of emotional detachment which he so eagerly sought.

With its emphasis on the material and pagan aspects of civilization, the artistic accomplishments of classical Antiquity reinforced Gautier's own marked preference and propensity for the visual and plastic conception of literary expression. The search for the hard and durable forms that would ensure the survival of poetic expression had already received the attention of such French Romanticists as Vigny in his "Bouteille à la mer" [Bottle in the sea].[14] Gautier's celebrated program poem, "L'Art," published in the 1857 edition [15] of Emaux et camées, proclaimed the exultant answer to the riddle with its exclamation that the eventual triumph of matter over the thwarted dreams and aspirations of the human mind could be realized through the work of art.

More than merely the plea for the artist to practice the care and control advocated by such classical reformers as Malherbe and Boileau, "L'Art" bespeaks behind the mask of its apparent formula for objectivity the kind of personal drama that lends the poem its own emotional strain and detectable lyrical dimension.

"L'Art" emerges as something considerably more than a carefully reasoned argument in favor of tightly controlled formal structures; it releases in ostensibly measured terms the publicly objective solution to a private, a personal dilemma:

> *Tout passe.—L'art robuste*
> *Seul à l'éternité,*
> *Le buste*
> *Survit à la cité,*
>
> *Et la médaille austère*
> *Que trouve un laboureur*
> *Sous terre*
> *Révèle un empereur.*
>
> *Les dieux eux-mêmes meurent.*
> *Mais les vers souverains*
> *Demeurent*
> *Plus forts que les airains.*

["Everything dies. Only the robust art lives forever: only the bust outlives the city. And the austere medallion which a ploughman discovers beneath the earth discloses the portrait of an emperor. The gods themselves die. But poems possess a sovereignty that remains stronger than that of bronzes."] The poem's ready recourse to the material substratum of Antiquity and the advocacy of a calm and pondered approach to artistic expression would receive the enthusiastic endorsement of the latter Parnassian poets as well as of the proponents of Art for Art's Sake.

Despite its predominant emphasis upon the necessity to observe the concrete manifestations of nature, Gautier's aesthetic attitude categorically rejected the view that art should aim at the mathematically precise rendering or reproduction of that reality. Rather, the kind of realistic expression that was sought was that begotten by the imaginative interpretation of observed facts. Art, then, was not the simple translation of any factually observed reality but rather its idealization. His

Histoire du Romantisme [History of Romanticism] reminds the poet of his obligation to transform his vision of the external world through the various forms, shades and colors at his disposal so that individual readers might be encouraged to articulate the dreams and the ideas that remain partially rooted and locked in such observations.[16]

Gautier openly railed at those artists who sought to mirror reality without any kind of intervention by dismissing their so-called realistic portraitures as cheap and valueless copy. The validity of artistic expression, he maintained, rested in its efficacity to detect and seize upon characteristic human traits, and to remove them from the ugly limitations of particularized contexts in order to transform them into statements of lasting beauty. Art is superior to nature, since beauty is something intrinsic to the poet or artist's creativity. In the "Salon de 1837," Gautier explains the creative genius of the painter, Cabat, in the following manner: "The model is hideous, yet the portrait has charm: how can that be? It is simply that art is something more beautiful, more powerful than nature; nature is stupid; it is not conscious of itself . . . it's something that is cheerless and colorless: it needs a creative soul to endow it with animation." [17] Since art emerges as something essentially superior to nature, it also asserts its independence from the social and moral constructions of specific men at given times and places.

The very concept of ideal beauty carried in its train strong suggestions of the rare, the sacred, and the mystical which appealed not only to Gautier but also to such a congener in Art for Art's Sake and Parnassianism as Leconte de Lisle. Anticipating the positivist framework of the 1850s and 1860s, Gautier found it convenient to replace the metaphysical postulates upon which rested the principal beliefs of the major Western religions with an aesthetic creed whose foundations were cemented in concrete reality.

Just as the later Positivists appended a mystique of

progress to their scientific orientation, the practitioners of Art for Art's Sake or literary Realism made a religion out of beauty and art. What both Baudelaire and Leconte de Lisle call sacred objects and inaccessible eternal essences in their respective poems, "Hymne à la beauté" [Hymn to beauty] and "Hypatie," Flaubert referred to a kind of mysticism and a refuge in a letter to Louise Colet, dated 14 August 1853: "Humanity despises us [artists]; we shall not serve its cause and we shall despise humanity because it seeks to wound us. Let us love one another in Art as the mystics love one another in God, and let everything fade before this love."

The great majority of the adepts of Art for Art's Sake and Parnassianism subscribed to the idea that art was absolute, an end in itself, and that the beauty which emanated from a work of art constituted something divine. Yet all remained mindful of the fact that the cult of beauty to which they had submitted their art was linked to the visible world rather than to the invisible one of their metaphysical counterparts in social Romanticism.

It would be a serious error to conclude that Gautier's aesthetic pronouncements in the prefaces to *Albertus* and *Mademoiselle de Maupin* elicited the kind of enthusiastic endorsement that made of Art for Art's Sake a major literary attitude during Louis-Philippe's July Monarchy. Gautier's conception of the autonomy of literature instigated instead the condemnation of virtually every significant partisan of social Romanticism. The Saint-Simonians dismissed his thesis with the categorical assertion that the only justification of art rests in its social function and in its contribution to the progress of civilization.

Liberal Catholics joined forces with such republican and socialist reformers as Louis Blanc and Proudhon to denounce Art for Art's Sake as the expression of a dangerous egotistical individualism. Scores of editorial comments in such notable journals as *Le Globe*, *L'Avenir*, the *Revue encyclopédique*, and *Revue ré-*

publicaine underscored the nefarious consequences implicit in an aesthetic code that concerned itself primarily with the purely descriptive portraiture of past civilizations.

In his *Esquisse d'une philosophie* [Outline for a philosophy] of 1840, Lamennais, with characteristic verve, argued quite simply: "Art is nothing less than the external form of ideas, the expression of religious dogma and of the dominant social principles of a given epoch. No form of art may exist within a vacuum; Art for Art's Sake is an absurdity." [18] Lamennais articulates, to a significant degree, the mood and temper of the July Monarchy that stirred thinkers and writers to commit themselves to the more pressing problems of social reform and revolution. Even such stalwart supporters of Parnassianism in the 1850s and 1860s as Leconte de Lisle, Louis Ménard, and Louis Bouilhet infused their writings with social and political propaganda in the years immediately preceding and following the Revolution of 1848. In short, Art for Art's Sake had succeeded in securing only the uncertain adherence of a small group of sympathizers during the regime of Louis-Philippe. The bitter disillusionment experienced by a great number of socially active thinkers and writers in 1851 inspired the kind of interest and enthusiasm in Art for Art's Sake that made of it a major literary reaction during the first decade of Louis-Napoleon's Second Empire.

With the suppression of freedom of the press and the elimination of universal suffrage during the opening years of the Second Empire, the most adamant republican and socialist advocates of reform were either quickly disorganized and exiled or deported. For socially committed poets like Hugo, determined to unleash their prophetic deprecations upon a repressive regime, only one choice was open to them: that of exile from their native France.

If the government of Louis-Napoleon openly encouraged useful and moral art, it also unwittingly favored the blossoming of Art for Art's Sake in the 1850s. The Second Empire tolerated with some condescension the aesthetic attitude of Art for Art's Sake only because it affirmed complete disassociation from all political as well as moral and social considerations. The truth of the matter, however, was that no literary or artistic stance enjoyed complete freedom from governmental interference and control.

The official condemnation of Flaubert's *Madame Bovary* and Baudelaire's *Les Fleurs du Mal* [The flowers of evil] in 1857, on the charges of outrage against public morality, served as a vivid reminder of the kind of censorship which was imposed. Nevertheless, the publication of such significant volumes as the *Emaux et Camées* of Gautier and the *Poèmes antiques* [Ancient poems] of Leconte de Lisle in 1852 as well as the fiction and poetry of Flaubert and Baudelaire constitutes sufficient justification for labelling Art for Art's Sake a major literary attitude of the 1850s. For lack of any more cohesive doctrine than the bold assertion of autonomy and independence from any outside influence, the principles underlying its aesthetic code came under the fairly steady attacks of both its enemies and of some of its own practitioners. In his 1852 essay on the poetry of Pierre Dupont,[19] Baudelaire questions the philosophy of noninvolvement in Art for Art's Sake: "The childish utopia of the school of Art for Art's Sake, in excluding ethical considerations and very frequently even passion, was necessarily sterile." Baudelaire's position with reference to the theory and practice of a purely autonomous literature is one both of sympathy and exasperation. Such poems in his *Fleurs du Mal* such as "La Beauté" [Beauty] and "Hymne à la beauté" are unquestionable endorsements of the formal and the philosophical principles of Art for Art's Sake. His 1859 appraisal of Gautier's art is nothing less than a panegyric of praise for autonomy in literature and a scathing denunciation of the concept of utility.[20] Yet, his study on "L'Ecole païenne" [The pagan school] in *L'Art romantique* unveiled again serious reservations which he entertained concerning the curtailment of personal expression in art and poetry.

The answer to Baudelaire's wavering position with respect to Art for Art's Sake is contained in his own poetry. While he espoused the cause of stricter forms in literary expression, he felt intimidated or limited by the heavy insistence upon a less personal and more plastic or concrete interpretation of reality. His increasing reliance upon unrestricted metaphors and images to convey the subjective allusiveness of musical sounds in his verse points to the development of future French Symbolism rather than to the orthodox expression of Art for Art's Sake or Parnassianism.

There existed few centers in the 1850s and early 1860s where the adept practitioners of the new literary aesthetic could rally to voice their common aims and iron out their respective differences of opinion. The most important of these rallying points was certainly the drawing room of Madame de Sabatier, dubbed "la présidente" by Gautier, where such writers as Flaubert, Gautier, Baudelaire, and Bouihlet met on consecutive Sundays in 1863 in order to read and discuss one another's works. The only major literary journal of note to recognize the merits of Art for Art's Sake in the 1850s was *L'Artiste*, whose direction and editorship Gautier assumed in 1856. The "Introduction," published in the 14 December 1856 issue, articulated the policy of autonomy in art and literature in the most explicit terms yet.

> We believe in the complete independence of art; art, for us, is not the means but the end. In our estimation, any artist who considers accomplishing something other than the beautiful in his work is not an artist at all. We have never understood the attitude that divorces ideas from their forms. A pleasing form is a pleasing idea, for what good is a form that expresses nothing?

The example of Gautier's sustained adherence to the principle of aesthetic autonomy during the years in which Art for Art's Sake remained overshadowed by social Romanticism through the first decade of the Second Empire records the history of the movement from its virtual inception to its eventual confrontation with Parnassianism in the mid-1860s. The differences which ultimately distinguished Art for Art's Sake from Parnassianism resulted from slight yet discernible shifts in emphasis and direction rather than from any serious divergence in orientation and ideology.

The very choice of the word, Parnassian, to describe fundamentally the continued practice of Art for Art's Sake in French poetry at first proved to be almost as controversial as it was arbitrary. An obscure poet, Marty-Laveaux, suggested the term to the editor, Alphonse Lemerre, who had agreed to publish a collection of poems, the majority of which shared a certain spiritual affinity with Art for Art's Sake, and for which anthology he eagerly sought a title. Leconte de Lisle voiced his bitter objection over the designation of Parnassian as entirely inappropriate and utterly absurd in the proposed context, yet the codirectors of the project, Catulle Mendès and Xavier de Ricard, ignored the objection,[21] and had the word incorporated into the title page in 1866, as, *Le Parnasse contemporain: recueil de vers nouveaux* [The contemporary Parnassus: an anthology of new verse].

The *Parnasse contemporain* of 1866 marked the first of three collections of poems claiming at least some vague allegiance to the attitude of Art for Art's Sake. The two remaining volumes appeared in 1871 and 1876 respectively. Taken compositely, the *Parnasse contemporain* affords the opportunity of surveying the poetry of some one hundred poets in the ten-year span from 1866 to 1876. Despite the conspicuous absence of any specific theory or doctrine, the *Parnasse contemporain* suggests, at least implicitly if not explicitly, a decided reaction to the exaggerated emotionalism and sentimentalism marring the French Romantic lyric. The one hundred poets represented in the anthologies are more urgently united in the solidarity of their artistic endeavor than they are in any specifically rigid attitude or school of thought. A partial listing of the wide range of poets most frequently encountered in the three volumes reveals the generous latitude in poetical outlook that motivated the organizers of the project. Such obviously prone practitioners of the plastic conception of Art for Art's Sake as Leconte de Lisle, Sully Prud-homme, and José-Maria de Heredia are interspersed with the more appropriately drawn exponents of Symbolism such as Baudelaire, Verlaine, and Mallarmé.[22]

If it could be convincingly argued that the *Parnasse contemporain* failed to advance any noticeably evolved aesthetic statement in behalf of a plastic Parnassianism that distinguished it significantly from the kind of Art for Art's Sake published in the 1850s, it might be equally maintained that no such theoretical purpose motivated the undertaking of Lemerre, Mendès, and Ricard. Indeed, Mendès spoke in unmistakably clear terms on the matter: "Parnassianism was born from the need to react to the license present in the poetry of Murger, Charles Bataille, Amédée Roland. . . . The Parnassian group is neither based on any theory nor on any aesthetic code."[23] While Mendès's assertion may strike us as debatable on several accounts, the defensive thrust behind his declaration betrays a sense of discomfort over the precarious state of poetry during the age of Positivism in France.

The various literary drawing rooms of such varied patrons as Nina de Villars, Madame de Ricard, Catulle Mendès, and Leconte de Lisle during the 1860s were constituted primarily to assert the need for autonomy in art, and to encourage and ensure the practice of poetic expression in a society predominantly concerned with more immediately useful values. Despite its claims at objectivity and its scientific orientation, the poetry of Art for Art's Sake and Parnassianism failed to enlist the interest and enthusiasm of any significantly substantial reading public. From 1851 to 1866, the editors of such prestigious firms as Michel Lévy, Charpentier, and Hetzel refused to consider any kind of poetry for publication. In their struggle against the contemptuous indifference of potential readers and the hostility of editors, the Parnassian poets understandably encouraged the interest which the well-known publisher, Alphonse Lemerre, had expressed over their plight. An admirer of the verse of Leconte de Lisle and Heredia, Lemerre invited the poets to read and discuss their poems at his bookstore at the passage Choiseul.

Eventually, Lemerre suggested to Xavier de Ricard that he abandon the directorship of his financially troubled journal, *L'Art,* to edit the series of poetry collections that was destined to be associated with the cause of Parnassianism. The appearance of the three instalments of the *Parnasse contemporain* represented, then, a considerable psychological victory for the poets whose verse purported no more than to celebrate formal beauty at a time when such poetry was being dismissed as gratuitous in favor of literary works that blatantly exploited scientific methodology for material ends. The rich variety in form as well as in thematic development rescued the *Parnasse contemporain* from any exclusive identification with any sectarian aesthetic philosophy. Public reaction to the three collections proved to be moderately successful. More important still, the poets in question benefited from both the public and critical exposure afforded them by the series.

Despite the absence of any theoretical argument in favor of Art for Art's Sake in the *Parnasse contemporain,* critics of the concept of autonomy in art nevertheless voiced their antipathy in a series of essays and parodies which, in some cases, served to elicit interest in the poets under attack. The succession of articles appearing in *Le Nain jaune* [The yellow dwarf] from 27 October to 14 November 1866 under the signature of Barbey d'Aurevilly constituted the most sustained virulent attack upon the literary current detectable in the first volume of the collection.

In general, Barbey reproaches the poets of the *Parnasse contemporain* for their conspicuous lack of belief and conviction, patently labeling them as dimunitive imitators: ". . . this bunch of monkeys who think they're men and who parade while beating their own drums on the stretched ass skins of the *Parnasse contemporain* . . . they're nothing more than poetical baboons and wistiti!" Barbey's burlesque, *Les Trente-sept médaillonets du Parnasse* [The thirty-seven small medallions of Parnassus], an obvious allusion to the thirty-seven poets represented in the 1866 edition, hardly succeeds as effective caricature since the portraits of such adherents of Parnassianism as Leconte de Lisle and Banville, for example, are difficult to distinguish.

An equally ambitious attack upon the attitudes manifest in Lemerre's anthologies was that undertaken by Alphonse Daudet and Paul Arène in the amusing pamphlet called, *Le Parnassiculet contemporain* [The lowbrowed contemporary Parnassus] in 1866 and 1872. The collaborators of this diverting spoof on such well-known personalities as Louis Ménard, Leconte de Lisle, and Heredia display considerable talent in protesting mostly the effrontery behind the conception of the anthologies: the arrogant supposition that only the included poets give the complete picture of French poetic expression. Paul Arène, by far the most successful contributor, wrote a thoroughly entertaining playlet entitled, *Gaël-Imar au grand pied* [Big-footed Gaël-Imar], an effective parody of Leconte de Lisle's manner with Scandinavian legend, and by far the most consistently amusing feature in the *Parnassiculet*. Whatever negative image it may have hoped to suggest, the critical reaction to Lemerre's anthologies underscored the growing influence which the poets of Art for Art's Sake had finally managed to exert on the French literary scene.

Despite the frequently biased accounts that detract from the credibility of Catulle Mendès's history of the literary movement during the 1860s, *La Légende du Parnasse contemporain* did corroborate the widely held assumption that the theoretical bases of Art for Art's Sake evolved somewhat loosely from the discussions in which its leading advocates participated at Alphonse Lemerre's bookstore at the passage Choiseul as well as in the several drawing rooms and literary workshops already mentioned. Under the official and effective leadership of Leconte de Lisle, the poets, increasingly referred to as Parnassians, sought to define the principles and attitudes that explained their common aesthetic outlook. The literary code of the Parnassian poets of the 1850s and 1860s is most easily deciphered in the program poems of its major practitioners and in the prefatory essays to Leconte de Lisle's collections of poems.[24] The purely technical aspects of Parnassianism are conveniently expressed in handbook form as *Petit Traité de poésie française* [Introductory treatise on French poetry], published by Théodore de Banville in 1872.

It is just as logical as it is ironic that the concepts of objectivity and ideal beauty that infiltrated the poetics of Parnassianism so thoroughly and effectively should be rooted in personal interpretations of man's predicament. Lyricism, the fusion of reason and feeling, purports to convey such personal reactions to human experience. However well disguised in the cloak of formal objectivity, the truly effective poetical expression of Parnassianism sought to infuse outwardly passive attitudes with a discernible, though controlled, personal dimension. Much maligned and misinterpreted by their detractors on the count of so-called impassibility, the leading Parnassian poets waged an almost relentless if somewhat unsuccessful battle to rid themselves of a charge they considered totally unjustified.

The designation resulted most probably from the obvious misreading of either Gautier or Glatigny's sonnets, "L'Impassible," in the 1871 edition of the *Parnasse contemporain.* Leconte de Lisle's abrupt reply to Jules Huret's query on impassibility and Parnassianism, subsequently recorded in the *Enquête sur l'évolution littéraire*, reveals the extent to which the term exasperated him: "When will they ever tire of that stupid story? Imagine, an impassive poet! I suppose that when one doesn't reveal how he buttons his trousers or divulge every aspect of his love life, one is called an impassive poet? The whole thing is stupid!"

In rejecting the excessive effusion of Romanticism, the Parnassians vowed to champion a tightly constructed and more impersonal lyricism steeped in the ready observation of concrete reality rather than in any carelessly devised and vaguely defined metaphysical attitude. In a probable allusion to Musset's parable of the pelican in "La Nuit de mai" [Night in May], Leconte de Lisle's sonnet, "Les Montreurs" [The Showmen], published in *Les Poèmes barbares* of 1862, decried the shameless practice of public personal confession in poetry as a prostitution of art. If "Les Montreurs" relegates such poets and such avowals to the barbaric tradition, the sonnet also succeeds admirably in defining the kind of tempered lyrical expression that was sought by the Parnassians. The two tercets conclude Leconte de Lisle's denunciation in the kind of impassioned language that blends ideas with personal feelings and conviction.

> *Dans mon orgueil muet, dans ma tombe sans gloire,*
> *Dussé-je m'engloutir pour l'éternité noire,*
> *Je ne te vendrai pas mon ivresse ou mon mal,*
>
> *Je ne livrerai pas ma vie à tes huées,*
> *Je ne danserai pas sur ton tréteau banal*
> *Avec tes histrions et tes prostituées.*

["Even if it meant my disappearance into the black abyss of eternity, in my muted pride and from my anonymous grave, I would not divulge my ecstasy or my disappointment to you. I refuse to disclose my private life to your public's clamor. I refuse to dance on your tawdry stage with your clowns and prostitutes."]

The aesthetic philosophy to which the majority of

Parnassian poets subscribed underlined the vast differences in personal outlook that distinguished them from the most prominent social Romantic poets. The latter proceeded to write their poems on the supposition that an accord between the individual and exterior nature could be achieved through the various conflicting cosmogonic explanations more replete with inspiration and emotion than with reason and factual observation. Social Romanticism was the poetry of the limitless possibilities of man. The Parnassians found the basis for their expression in the sober and precise observation of nature and history and tended to project the limitations of human design and accomplishment in the kind of verse which tacitly suggested a pondered and quiet resignation to such limits.

The fact of the matter was that the Parnassian objection to the preposterous claims of social Romanticism came, for the most part, on the heels of the failure of the 1848 Revolution and the attendant fiasco of the short-lived Second Republic. Thus, the majority of Parnassian poets tended to judge the unlimited optimism of Romantic aspiration from the optic of a recent historical event as well as from the obvious sense of disillusionment they experienced as a result of such a drastic event. The quasi-metaphysical tinge and the detectable tone of anticipation present in the writings of Baudelaire, Leconte de Lisle, and Louis Ménard in 1848, for example, constitute fairly indisputable evidence that these future partisans of Art for Art's Sake and Parnassianism shared in the enthusiasm that infused social Romanticism during the last years of the July Monarchy.

From the perspective of the ensuing Second Empire, the Parnassians countered the hopeful aspirations of a prior Romanticism with a sober, if not pessimistic, appraisal of the human predicament that resulted from their close observation of fact and reality. If social Romanticism proclaimed an inspired mystique of progress and energy, Parnassianism voiced a discouraging conviction of the futility of effort in modern times.

The claims of social Romanticism surfaced in an undisguised individualism and subjectivity; the assertions
of Parnassianism resulted from the methodical control of significantly more objective observation of external nature. The difference divorcing Romanticism
from Parnassianism, then, was one of method or approach rather than one of ideological attitude. The
latter emerged the result or the consequence of the
methodology employed.

Leconte de Lisle's preface to the *Poèmes antiques*
of 1852 issued an unmistakable reprimand to the Romanticists whose lyrical expression displayed the woe-
ful lack of any kind of method or cohesiveness, and
concluded somewhat caustically: ". . . you were incapa-
ble of mouthing anything else but your own inanity."
From the vantage point of the aftermath of the 1848
Revolution, Leconte de Lisle defines the shift in orientation and methodology that will rescue poetry from its
ridiculous presumption. The definition that he ad-
vances betrays the personal sense of frustration and
futility which he feels when confronted by the contemporary situation of 1852.

> In these uncertain times, the most sensible and
> reasonable minds stop to consult one another. The
> others do not even know where they come from or
> where they are going: in their haste and blindness,
> they subscribe to whatever feverish agitation they en-
> counter. Only the former are conscious of the tran-
> sitory character of their age and of the fatal demands
> it may make on them. We are a generation of
> scholars; the spontaneous world of instinct, so abun-
> dantly in evidence during our youth, has been with-
> drawn from us: such is the irreparable fact. Poetry,
> expressed as an art form, will no longer preoccupy it-
> self with heroic deeds nor will it inspire men to social
> action because the power of its sacred language has
> been diminished. As in every period of literary deca-
> dence, in the desperate hope of discovering some latent

form of heroism or some remnant of virtue, poetry has become reduced to expressing only petty personal impressions punctuated by an arbitrary use of neologisms. In short, poetry has become enslaved to the caprice of personal taste, and it is no longer fit to teach man.

Leconte de Lisle's essay has the thrust of a virtual manifesto advocating the complete reform of poetic expression. It is replete with allusions to such notions as antiquarianism, antimodernism, impersonalism, antiutilitarianism and scientific orientation which eventually worked their way into the fabric of the Parnassian aesthetic. Considerably more than a prospectus on the impersonalized verse that he attempted to achieve in the *Poèmes antiques*, the introductory article constitutes a summation of the type of indoctrination which gradually infiltrated the minds of eager disciples who frequented the literary workshop of Leconte de Lisle on the boulevard des Invalides.

By the sheer aggressiveness of its tone, the preface to the *Poèmes antiques* may be construed as a categorical breach with social Romanticism. In general, the essay received the approbation of the sympathizers of Art for Art's Sake. In a letter to Louise Colet, however, Flaubert took exception both to Leconte de Lisle's advocacy of a return to the study and emulation of Greek antiquity, and to his heavy insistence upon formal perfection: ". . . we must not attempt a return to Hellenism but rather content ourselves to borrowing its methods and procedures. There are more things to art than well-written lines and polished surfaces." [25] In the epigram to his study of six French poets, *Les Poètes contemporains*, collected and published in the posthumous volume, *Derniers poèmes*, Leconte de Lisle articulated the principle that crowned his entire aesthetic outlook: "The world of beauty, the only objective of Art, comprises in itself an infinite which can have no possible contact with any type of inferior conception."

It was the nineteenth-century critic, Jules Lemaître, who most accurately defined Leconte de Lisle's Greek antiquarianism as the union of the two strongest sentiments that came to dominate his life and work: the love of plastic beauty and a sense of disenchantment with contemporary existence.[26] De Lisle's ultimate disillusionment with the vaguely prophetic Fourierism to which he had subscribed as well as the personal dissatisfaction he experienced emotionally brought him to the brink of complete disgust and exasperation as early as 1845. What he lacked was precisely the sense of purpose, direction and cohesion that he had so urgently sought. He found it gradually in the formulation of the conclusion that happiness resided in the love and cult of an imperishable beauty that was conceived as impersonally as possible.

The concept of permanence, alien to the world which in its everyday activity underscored the transitoriness of existence, became associated with the concrete manifestations bequeathed by past civilizations. Whatever corroboration Leconte de Lisle may have required for his thesis, it was more than abundantly supplied in the person and thought of Louis Ménard, Hellenist philologist and ardent champion of Greek art and stoical philosophy. His *Prométhée délivré* [Prometheus unchained] and *Rêveries d'un païen mystique* [Musings of a mystical pagan] preached the superiority of pagan Greek polytheism over Christianity because it encouraged the harmonious union of religion with philosophy and poetry, and thus achieved a measure of success in satisfying the most pressing requirements of man's aspirations.

In Leconte de Lisle's view, this doctrine corresponded closely to his own interpretation of reality, and as early as 1846, under the friendly tutelage of Louis Ménard, he began in earnest his study of the Greek language and civilization. Both Leconte de Lisle and Louis Ménard figured prominently in the subsequent literary movement that favored a revival of the contemplation and imitation of Greek antiquity. De Lisle's conception of Hellenism constituted one of the principal cornerstones upon which he constructed the most important part of the aesthetic code of Parnassianism. The antiquarianism he advocated gave fuller dimension to such notions as antiutilitarianism, impersonalism, scientific orientation and the idealization of beauty which eventually became part and parcel of the outlook of the major Parnassian poets.

In large measure, the preface to *Poèmes et poésies* of 1855 may be construed as Leconte de Lisle's attempt to justify the Hellenism which served to detach him from Romanticism and to set him in opposition to Hugo. In an obvious reply to Flaubert's objection to his stated preference for Antiquity over modernism, de Lisle makes no effort to disguise his contempt for the latter: "I would like to think—and may I be forgiven for making this monstrous comparison—that the work of Homer will be significantly more appreciated in the history of humanity than the work of Blanqui." Leconte de Lisle's return to antiquarianism constituted more than a refuge or retreat from which he could indulge in the quiet contemplation of perfection in art, it also provided him with the vantage point he needed to vent his disgust for the ugliness and neobarbarianism of a disdainful nineteenth century. The utilitarian spirit of Comte's evolved Positivism, for all of its scientific pretensions, has created a world devoid of poetry. He unleashes all of his venom against the heresy of didacticism in art and literature.

The various hymns and odes inspired by the discoveries of steam and electric telegraphy only stir my most mediocre sentiments, and all these didactic periphrases which have nothing to do with art tend to convince me that poets are becoming more and more useless to modern societies. Doubtless, poets have suffered in every age, but even in the most unfavorable times, in exile or in madness, the merit of their genius remained undisputed and incontestable. But the moment is rapidly drawing near when they shall be forced to cease writing to avoid their own intellectual demise. I am thoroughly convinced that such will soon be the inevitable plight of all those who refuse to prostitute the nature of their vocation for the benefit of the monstrous alliance between poetry and industry. It is because of the natural repulsion which we experience for that which destroys us that I loathe the times in which I live.

De Lisle equates modernism with barbarianism and decries the utilitarian exigencies which have stripped humanity of its sense of the ideal. He would replace modernism with Greek antiquity, restore the Greek temples and resurrect the menagerie of Greek gods because he may attest to their survival in the lasting beauty bequeathed them by their sculptors and poets. The alliance between sculpture and poetry, taken up again by Théophile Gautier in his manifesto poem, "L' Art," in 1857, best ensures the idea of an enduring and permanent work of art.

The adoption of the cult of Hellenism by such poets as Leconte de Lisle, Louis Ménard, Théodore de Banville, Sully Prudhomme, and Heredia exposed through indirection the pessimistic attitude that punctuated their aesthetic philosophy. Their common stance is that of rejection of the aspirations and values which dominated the era in which they lived. The subject matter and the themes associated with past cultures afforded the Parnassians the perfect opportunity of divorcing themselves officially from the social and historical contexts of the day with precisely the kind of detachment they desired. The poetic and artistic exploitation of antiquarianism catapulted them psychologically into an ambience far removed from the practical contingencies of their own, and favored the pursuit of ideals more attuned with their personal aspirations. Their consequent idealization of Antiquity provides an implicit though nonetheless eloquent contrast with the pettiness of modern times. The particular manner in which they approached ancient art and civilization endowed their poetry with the kind of exoticism that rescued them ultimately from succumbing to feelings of abject despair. Their antiquarianism, then, constituted a refuge and a retreat from the crass considerations of a modern society bereft of any meaningful idealism. To a significant degree, the various interpretations of Antiquity infused Parnassian poetry with a decidedly personal and lyrical flavor.

The Parnassian preference for essentially static civilizations over modernism projects a profound sense of pessimism into their verse which is frequently more than readily discernible. The 1850s signal the beginning of literary decadence and of social degeneracy since purely dated issues, rooted in the relativity of pragmatic principles, have succeeded in dominating French institutions at the noticeably painful exclusion of all idealism. In a sonnet composed for its inclusion in the *Poèmes barbares*, Leconte de Lisle denounces the preoccupations of his contemporaries in unmistakable terms. "Aux Modernes" [To the moderns] effectively uses the kind of visual imagery that appeals vividly to the imagination in a blunt condemnation of modern man's empty vision of existence:

> Votre cervelle est vide autant que votre sein,
> Et vous avez souillé ce misérable monde
> D'un sang si corrompu, d'un souffle si malsain,
> Que la mort germe seule en cette boue immonde.
>
> Hommes, tueurs de Dieux, les temps ne sont pas loin
> Où, sur un grand tas d'or vautrés dans quelque coin,
> Ayant rongé le sol nourricier jusqu'aux roches,
>
> Ne sachant faire rien ni des jours ni des nuits,
> Noyés dans le néant des suprêmes ennuis,
> Vous mourrez bêtement en emplissant vos poches.

["Your brain is as empty as your breast, and you have contaminated this wretched world with blood so depraved and a climate that is so unhealthy, that only

death germinates from this unspeakably filthy mire.
Men, killers of gods, the time is not far off when,
sprawled out in some corner on huge mounds of gold,
having corroded even the rocks of the earth that fostered
you, and not knowing what to do with your days and
nights, drowned in the nothingness of a colossal bore-
dom, you shall die stupidly while stuffing your pock-
ets."] De Lisle's ominous predictions of the consequences of a mindlessly utilitarian society are invested
with the kind of prophetic tone that penetrated the
Parnassians's rejection of contemporary civilization.

The striking contrast between the splendors kindled
by the imagination and the painful limits imposed by
reality led the Romantic poets to articulate their dilemma over man's predicament in terms that frequently
betrayed the pretension of personally evolved cosmogonic explanations. There are many instances in Romantic poetry which point to an intimate alliance with
metaphysics. For the most part, Romantic optimism
stemmed from the intuitively founded conviction that
the poet, serving as intermediary between God and
man, could successfully resolve the cosmic enigma of
human destiny, and enlighten man spiritually and socially through his diligent guidance and leadership. Social Romantic expression took frequent recourse in the
vague and ethereal qualities of language that was more
ideally suited to translate the crystallized *rêveries* of
the poets in question.

Parnassianism, on the other hand, chose to approach
the same dilemma of the ideal and the real through the
projection of an attitude that made specific reference to
systematic study and the factual observation of the external forms of reality. The recorded efforts of man in
past civilizations to find the answer to the riddle of the
human enigma convinced the Parnassian poets of its
insolubility. In a manner reminiscent of Senancour's
protagonist, *Obermann,* they concluded that the understanding of the essence of human nature would never
be achieved, and adopted an attitude that resembled

stoicism. Since man could not aspire to the realization of any metaphysical knowledge in human existence, he would find solace in the observation and contemplation of the surfaces and appearances of a world that manifested itself in purely plastic and material terms. From such a confrontation with the external features of nature, the Parnassian poets hoped to extract an appreciation of the ideal and the beautiful. The positive and material aspect of their poetry proceeds logically from an emphatic interest in the outward aspects of reality. The philosophical implication in their stance echoes the following line from Baudelaire's "L'Amour du mensonge" [The love of the lie], inserted in the 1861 edition of the *Fleurs du Mal*: "Masque ou décor, salut! J'adore ta beauté." ["Mask or prop, I hail you! I love your beauty."]

In their common resolve to eschew the arbitrariness and the pretentiousness of the social Romanticists, the Parnassian poets publicized their intention to establish poetry upon the more objective foundation of a scholarly representation of beauty in art. Leconte de Lisle's preface to the *Poètes contemporains* in 1864 described the poet's procedure as follows: "He perceives things immediately and much further, much higher, much more profoundly than anyone else because he contemplates the ideal through visible beauty, and contains and enshrines it in his own precise language."

The poet's task, then, was to seek out the manifestations of a lasting beauty residing in the concrete reality which he observed, and to transpose his sense of beauty in verse that tended, for the most part, toward the descriptive. The Parnassian poet meticulously avoided the arrangement of ideas with a view to prove a point, and attempted to mask his personal stance with objectivity. The ideals which he sought to impart were those most closely identifiable with the material texture of the universe rather than with any spiritual value which he may have personally derived from the suppositions of metaphysical considerations.

It may be safely said that both the Parnassians and the Positivists, in their admitted preference for the kind of evidence which resulted from factual observation, asserted the supremacy of a material world. Such a view, of course, tended to predispose them toward materialistic interpretations of the human predicament but did not rule out the possibility of their private subscription to a spiritually oriented explication of man. Like the Positivists, the Parnassian poets excluded the realm of the spiritual from their preoccupations because it could be neither controlled nor verified by factual observation.

It is not altogether accurate to assume that the Parnassian poets refrained completely from imparting certain points of view and from infusing their verse with an almost mystical declaration of faith in their own aesthetic principle. The truth of the matter was that their rejection of the paradoxical Romantic explanation of man's enigma—that his quest for unity is achieved in the duality of matter and spirit—led them directly to their conception of the cult of idealized beauty. The quest for an ideal transcending the contingencies of nature and daily existence became entangled in the unfounded dogmas of a personally inspired religion for the Romanticists.

The Parnassian poets in their desire to link the ideal with the real associated their quest with art. The cult of idealized beauty in art rescued them from the deteriorating aspects of a pessimism that stifled both life and action, and inspired them to seek a partial solution to man's dilemma in art. What the Parnassians actually meant by their avowed cult of the beautiful may be deciphered in Leconte de Lisle's poem, "La Vénus de Milo," inspired in large measure by Théodore de Banville's "A la Muse grecque" [To the Greek muse], and published in the 1852 edition of the *Poèmes antiques*:

> Du bonheur impassible ô symbole adorable,
> Calme comme la Mer en sa sérénité,

Nul sanglot n'a brisé ton sein inaltérable,
Jamais les pleurs humains n'ont terni ta beauté.

. . . .

Iles, séjour des Dieux! Hellas, mère sacrée!
Oh! que ne suis-je né dans le saint Archipel,
Aux siècles glorieux où la Terre inspirée
Voyait le Ciel descendre à son premier appel!

["Oh adorable symbol of impassive Beauty, as calm as
the sea in its serenity, no sob has disturbed your unalterable breast, and never have human tears tarnished
your beauty. Islands, sojourn of the gods! Hellas, sacred
mother! Oh, why could I not have been born in the
holy Archipelago during that glorious era when an inspired earth could see the heavens descend at its first
appeal."]

These stanzas constitute more than a mere visual
celebration of the virginal purity and harmony which
the contemplation of the statue of Venus of Milo inspires in the poet. The qualifying adjectives, which follow one another in fairly rapid succession, *impassive*,
calme and *inaltérable*, emphasize the Parnassian conception of ideal beauty while they also convey the poet's
impression of the superiority of Greek antiquity. The
beauty of Venus escapes the disfigurement of time and
passion, and carries in its train the suggestion of permanence, the artist's material embodiment of the notion of eternity in a lasting work of art. De Lisle's admiration for ancient Greece is punctuated by a nostalgic regret for not having known Antiquity first-hand.
The poem conjures the contemporary reader, obsessed
with a preoccupation for the spiritual, to suspend his
religious interpretation of humanity sufficiently long to
appreciate the impassive happiness derived from the
contemplation of such idealized beauty.

Both by their theoretical pronouncements and by
their poetic practice, the Parnassians enabled the ma-
terialization of art to become increasingly more erudite
and systematic. Like the plastic arts, their poetry at-

tempted to represent external reality without too many subjective rearrangements to illustrate a purely personal reaction or point of view. Only representational art was pure and durable for it sought the reproduction of those characteristic qualities in nature which successfully managed to elude the fate reserved the banal and quickly dated theses of utilitarian works. In representational art, the writer's poetic imagination made willing reference to fact and experience in order to capture the salient features of reality and to avoid insistence on any given subjective viewpoint.

Such art, buttressed by truth, infused itself with a sense of vitality that enhanced the chances for its survival. If it may be said that the leading Parnassians sought the corroboration of science and experience, it should also be underlined that they campaigned just as vigorously to keep their poetry intact from any subservience to science. What interested them was the methodology of science which they sought to implement in various fashions in their own poetry. Because the reigning "Scientism" and the Positivist spirit of the time lent itself so readily to the designs of an officially sanctioned utilitarianism, such practitioners of an allegedly pure and untainted art as the Parnassian poets voiced their suspicion of science, and distinguished between a disinterested scientific method and pragmatic science.[27]

In his essay on Théophile Gautier in the *Art romantique,* Baudelaire pointed out the consequences reserved for literature if any strict alliance was made with science and ethics: "At the risk of its failure and demise, poetry cannot become assimilated to science or to morality." As the most influential proponent of Parnassianism, Leconte de Lisle underscored the common denominators between art and science with respect to morality and encouraged a cautious *rapprochement* between poetry and scientific method.

What Leconte de Lisle sought in the *rapprochement* which he urged was the achievement of a more precise conception of reality through the critical faculties sharpened by a controlled, scientific approach to poetry. The scientific or scholarly approach to lyricism would endow poetry with a more universally identifiable picture of reality by keeping in check, but not squelching, the important role played by the imagination in works of art.

The most successful poetry of the Parnassian movement achieves such an objective. Parnassian art, then, aimed at translating the artist's own predispositions within the contained limits which objectivity and impersonality imposed in its expression. Théodore de Banville in his *Petit Traité de poésie française* [Introductory treatise on French poetry], published in 1872, fathoms the objectives of Parnassian poetry as follows: "Your poetry will express your mind and heart, and we will see clearly reflected your vices, your failings and weaknesses. You will perhaps manage to deceive some men, but your hypocrisy will never succeed in fooling the Muse."

The poet's mission is to restore art to its original purity. The Parnassian poets took from science its method in order to rejuvenate art and proclaim its ideal which had for so long been obscured by purely dated and pragmatic considerations. The aesthetic code to which the majority of French Parnassians subscribed did not outlaw all form of action from poetic expression. The Parnassian creed warned its practitioners, however, of the dangers and risks engendered in close involvement with present issues. It favored the scholarly study of past civilizations and traditions so that the inevitable laws upon which rest the future of mankind might be divulged through lasting works of art. Parnassianism sought to remind poets of the veritable aims of their art. Leconte de Lisle explained this ambition in the preface to the *Poèmes antiques*:

Art and science, separated for so long by divergent intellectual reactions, must aim to link themselves close together. Art has expressed the primitive revelation of the ideal contained in exterior reality, while science has calmly analyzed the poetic claim in order to expose it more clearly. But art has lost its intuitive spontaneity, or rather, it has exhausted it. It is now for science to infuse art with a renewed appreciation of its forgotten traditions so that it may be enabled to crystallize them in appropriate formal expression.

It was precisely the mutual *rapprochement* advocated between art and science, and detectable in the poetic practice of its leading exponents that ultimately distinguished Parnassianism from the kind of Art for Art's Sake that is best characterized in French poetry by Théophile Gautier.

The flexibility and the freedom with which the Parnassian poets evolved their aesthetic code prevented their discussions on art from disintegrating into a mere laboratory or workshop with the obvious objective of grinding out the theoretical aspects for set verse forms. The only attempt to impose official doctrine on the art of versification proved unsuccessful. Théodore de Banville's *Petit Traité de poésie française*, published only in 1872, constituted little more than a handbook on versification that remained ignored by the Parnassian poets except for Glatigny.

The truth of the matter was that the various poets exercised their right to develop the kind of verse form that suited their disposition, the only rule enforced for each one being "that each verse must show that it has been well thought out and chiseled." An examination of the poetry of the major collections of Banville, Prudhomme, de Lisle, and Heredia shows that Parnassian verse forms run the gamut from Romantic looseness to the classical regularity sought by de Lisle.

The Franco-Prussian War and the ensuing Commune of 1871 brought about the decline of Parnassianism and its eventual dispersion. The urgent sense of struggle for personal and national existence pervaded the movement with principles that proved incompatible with its avowed aesthetic attitude. Many of the poems written by such diverse figures as Banville, Gautier, Prud-homme, and de Lisle during 1871 are little more than calls to patriotic action.

The fall of Sedan and the subsequent siege of Paris only served to reinforce, however, de Lisle's political disdain and contemptuous regard for the times in which he lived. De Lisle and Heredia, notably, would continue to publish verse that conformed to the code that had been evolved during the 1860s. Other poets like Théodore de Banville, for example, defected from the aesthetic of Parnassianism for personal and ideological reasons. It may be safely concluded that both Art for Art's Sake and Parnassianism rose in idealistic reaction to the social Romanticism of the 1830s. The formal reforms instituted by Art for Art's Sake and Parnassianism were destined to survive in the Symbolist verse that dominated French poetry after the Franco-Prussian War.

2

Théophile Gautier and the Quest for Objectivity

Examination of Théophile Gautier's lyrical production from the first *Poésies* of 1830 to the augmented edition of *Emaux et camées* of 1857 reveals the poet's remarkably sustained attempt to check a personally evolved pessimism from deteriorating into an abjectly nihilistic reaction to human experience. Gautier's obsessive fear of death asserted itself with such categorical force by 1830 that it instilled in him contrary impulses to flight and immobility.[1] The theory of Art for Art's Sake which he subsequently worked out responded just as importantly to the requirements of his emotional tendencies as to the aesthetic ideal which he conceived. His retreat into an attitude that preached the independence of art from practical considerations resulted, in large measure, from a fatalistic interpretation of reality that underscored the inevitable transitoriness of all human values. Even before his reaction to the aftermath of the July Revolution of 1830, this sense of fatalism predicted his disillusionment in society since it rejected a priori the argument of possible human perfectibility.

To achieve mental stability, Gautier took refuge in the kind of inner calm that ostensibly derived from an assumed impassibility and from virtual withdrawal from the more enervating issues of the time. His consequent definition of Art for Art's Sake advocated the quest of formal perfection in art, the idealization of the discernible appearances of reality rather than reality it-

self. The contemplation of exterior reality and the idealized reproduction of its beauty led to the discovery of a
permanent texture in existence, and satisfied the creative urge to transform nature through art. The impas-
siveness with which Gautier attempted the artistic recreation of nature betrays a noticeable artificial quality
that invests his most memorable poems with an undeniable if controlled lyrical dimension. If his aesthetic
attitude contributed in dominating the emotional and
pessimistic substratum of his lyricism, it did not elimi-
nate all allusions to a more personally conceived inner
reality. In the 15 October 1922 issue of the *Mercure de
France*, Gabriel Brunet underlined the double facet of
Gautier's verse in the following terms: "His lyricism
is, in the main, linked to his own philosophical tendencies. It is a poetry of forgetfulness basking in the charm
of external appearances." [2]

The genesis of Gautier's doctrine of Art for Art's
Sake, as a corrective to his own predispositions to nihil-
ism, may be traced to Hugo's celebrated attack on classicism in the *Préface à Cromwell* of 1829, and to the
publication of his collection, *Les Orientales*, in the
same year. In the critical miscellany of 1833, *Les
Grotesques*, Gautier, with remarkable astuteness, re-
appraised the works of such divergent writers as Villon, Scarron, and Cyrano de Bergerac from the perspective of Hugo's thesis on the coexistence of the sublime
and grotesque in art and reality. His *Poésies* of 1830
and *España* of 1845, for all their heavy Romantic atmosphere, display a discernible if not altogether successful attempt to imitate the kind of visual beauty and
the variety in poetic expression so prominently in evidence in *Les Orientales*. Hugo's conception of the sublime and the grotesque, and the importance he ascribed
to local color in his evocations of the Middle East contributed significantly in reorienting Gautier's Romanticism toward the more minute observation of external
reality. P. E. Charvet has aptly described this occurrence
as Gautier's rejection of Romanticism in its profound-

est sense.[3] What the poet of *Emaux et camées* discovered in *Les Orientales* was the means by which he could extract himself successfully from his egocentric predicament without compromising his artistic integrity. In his view, the contemplation of external reality and the pleasing rendering of its formal beauty in visual and concrete terms ensured the artist's perpetuation.

Whatever hopes Gautier may have temporarily associated with the advent of Louis-Philippe and the July Monarchy, he quickly dispelled in a program poem containing an analogy to Dante's *Inferno*. The seventh sonnet of the *Poésies* records Gautier's resolve to disassociate himself from social Romanticism ironically enough in terms that pay its future champion a singular tribute:

> Avec ce siècle infâme, il est temps que l'on rompe;
> Car à son front damné le doigt fatal a mis
> Comme aux portes d'enfer: Plus d'espérance! Amis,
> Ennemis, peuples, rois, tout nous joue et nous trompe.
>
> . . . .
>
> Cependant en juillet, sous le ciel indigo,
> Sur les pavés mouvants ils ont fait des promesses
> Autant que Charles dix avait ouï de messes!
>
> Seule, la poésie incarnée en Hugo
> Ne nous a pas déçus, et de palmes divines,
> Vers l'avenir tournée, ombrage nos ruines.

"It is time that we break with this unspeakable century for destiny has inscribed on its doomed forehead as on the gates of hell: No more hope! Friends, enemies, the common people, kings, everyone takes advantage of us and deceives us. Nevertheless, from the barricades under the blue July sky, they made as many promises as Charles X heard masses. Only poetry as it is incarnated in Hugo has not disappointed us, and has overshadowed our ruins with divine laurels turned toward the future."

Despite Hugo's position of leadership in French social Romanticism after 1843, Gautier refrained, out of a deep sense of indebtedness, from any open criticism of him until his 1868 preface to an edition of Baudelaire's complete works published by Michel Lévy. Be that as it may, the seventh sonnet of *Poésies* underscored his personal disposition toward the political and social machinations of a society which he sought to divorce from his aesthetic preoccupations.

The prevailing tendency even among such distinguished critics as Albert Thibaudet and André Gide to judge Gautier solely as the poet of exterior reality [4] has led to the widespread assumption that Art for Art's Sake is necessarily limited by the portrayal and representation of the surface world of fact. Such a view, of course, may be partially corroborated by a superficial reading of Gautier's program poem, "L'Art," and by the prefatory manifesto to *Mademoiselle de Maupin*, but an examination of the poet's practice in such collections as *Poésies* and *Emaux et camées* underscores the inaccuracy or incompleteness of the observation.

Despite his resolve to contain the expression of his personal emotions behind the mask of apparent impassibility, Gautier frequently infused his poetry with a Romantic background or atmosphere that invested it with a distinctive personal flavor that was a prevalent characteristic residing in the poetry during the period in which he wrote. The fact of the matter was that Gautier's verse, even after the publication of his manifesto on Art for Art's Sake in the preface to *Albertus* in 1832, continued to share in many points of contact with the traditions most commonly associated with Romanticism. The general tones detectable in his lyricism run a wide gamut from the fantastic and grotesque conjurations in *Poésies, Poésies diverses* and *La Comédie de la mort* [The comedy of death] to the exotic and plastic evocations in *Emaux et camées*. The motifs which permeate his poetic production work their way into such notable narratives as *La Morte amoureuse* [The beloved dead lady] in 1836, *Roman de la momie* [Story of the mummy] in 1858 to *Spirite* in 1865.

The evident Romantic atmosphere pervading a large number of his poems more often than not conformed to the various shades of his personal sentiments at the moment of composition. Many of these poems may strike us a little better than obvious poetical exercises, and the Romantic mood which emanates from such pieces would hardly survive any serious comparison with the better poetry of Hugo and Musset, for example. Yet, a brief examination of the manner in which Gautier sought to master his verbal expression and control his personal feelings in the verse he published from 1830 to 1857 affords us the best opportunity of studying his evolution from Romanticism to Art for Art's Sake.

Gautier's advocacy of Art for Art's Sake stemmed from a personal need to reform the purely formal and technical aspects of his early poetry as well as from a gnawing pressure to resolve his ideological and aesthetic dilemma. The first sonnet in *Poésies*, published in 1830, lays bare Gautier's deficiency in successfully evoking the kind of melancholic response to nature that punctuated the best known poems of Lamartine and Musset:

> Aux vitraux diaprés des sombres basiliques,
> Les flammes du couchant s'éteignent tour à tour;
> D'un âge qui n'est plus que précieuses reliques,
> Leurs dômes dans l'azur tracent un noir contour;
>
> Et la lune paraît, de ses rayons obliques
> Argentant à demi l'aiguille de la tour,
> Et les derniers rameaux des pins mélancoliques
> Dont l'ombre se balance et s'étend alentour.
>
> Alors les vibrements de la cloche qui tinte,
> D'un monde aérien semblent la voix éteinte,
> Qui, par le vent portée, en ce monde parvient;
>
> Et le poète assis près des flots, sur la grève,
> Ecoute ces accents fugitifs comme un rêve,
> Lève les yeux au ciel, et triste se souvient.

["Against the variegated stained-glass windows of the darkened cathedrals, the flaming rays of the setting sun die out one by one; from an age that is no more than a precious memory, their domes cast a black outline against the blue sky. And the moon appears, its oblique light casting half a silver shimmer on the uppermost point of the tower, while the last branches of the melancholic pines are shrouded in a quivering shadow. Then the sounds of the tolling bell, like the muted voice from an aerial domain, are carried by the wind and thus reach our ears. And the poet, sitting on the beach near the waves, listens to these fugitive words as if in a dream. He lifts his eyes heavenward, and sadly, he remembers."]

In this sonnet, Gautier fails satisfactorily to blend the external landscape description with the personal sentiment that he would wish to convey. The quatrains and the tercets produce jarring and intrusive effects upon one another, and reveal the poem's conspicuous lack of technical and thematic cohesion. Gautier's ready reference to such standard Romantic imagery as the cathedrals against the backdrops of setting suns, and the moon casting its eerie shadows upon the black pine trees does not endow the sonnet with any kind of convincing intrinsic reality. The sonnet does not evoke a sense of melancholia simply because the poet spells the term outright in a qualitative manner. The cathedrals, the nocturnal evocation, the funereal tolling of the bell, and the poet stating sadly his recollection of a past event emerge as just so many disparate elements without conjuring up effectively and memorably any feeling of alienation and melancholy. The poet's attitude, alluded to in the last tercet, is conveyed in such vague language so as not to derive from the preceding two quatrains and the tercet. The compositional structure of the sonnet points out the type of technical difficulties which Gautier would seek to overcome in poems more immediately related to his conception of Art for Art's Sake. The first sonnet of *Poésies* invites comparison on both a thematic and technical level with the opening poem of *Emaux et camées*, "Affinités secrètes: madrigal panthéiste," as well as with Baudelaire's "La Vie antérieure" in *Les Fleurs du Mal*.

If such varied collections as *Poésies*, *Albertus*, and *La Comédie de la mort* exploited such obvious Romantic themes as the fear of death and the transitoriness of human existence, there may be detected in a growing number of poems a discernible improvement over Gautier's earliest sonnets. *Albertus* contains many descriptive passages that unveil Gautier's undeniable talent for the complex delineation of perspective. The fantastic elements that invest this long narrative poem with a Faustian atmosphere are punctured by frequent sketches and tableaus that stand as veritable models of precision in descriptive technique. Most of the imagery to which the poet has recourse possesses a distinctive pictorial quality that foreshadows the more successful visual evocations in *Emaux et camées*.

Whatever else, *Albertus* bears unmistakable testimony to Gautier's improvement in handling the technical aspects of narrative poetry. Personal reactions and sentiments remain subdued as controlled subjective colorations that never obtrude offensively into the account. They are, for the most part, skilfully integrated into the fantastic atmosphere of the poem with the kind of adroit adjustment that lend the narrative a fairly sustained dramatic intensity.

Despite the triteness of its theme, *Albertus* nonetheless unveils Gautier's increased awareness of his need to control the formal ingredient of his verse in order to keep in check his subjective response and obtain the kind of impassibility that he wished to project. As such, *Albertus* points to the direction of *Emaux et camées* more than to the first *Poésies*.

The poem, "Pastel," written in 1835 and subsequently published in the 1838 edition of *Poésies diverses*, illustrates to which extent Gautier was capable of maneuvering the formal and subjective aspects of his poetry in order to conform more closely to the spirit of his doctrine of Art for Art's Sake. In "Pastel," the reader may readily detect the kind of collaboration between poet and painter that took place in order to achieve through a subtle transposition such a highly evocative reminiscence of eighteenth-century gallantry. The poem is all the more remarkable for the discretion with which it suggests a theme that virtually haunted the poet and led him to several instances of emotional excess in the earlier *Poésies*. The use of the decasyllabic line is both appropriate and clever since the verse form was prominently associated with the eighteenth century, and since it allowed the poet to submerge his personal reaction into a sufficiently remote period of history so as to convey the overall impression of contained emotion.

Each line is adroitly broken up after the fourth syllable by the caesura with the result that the first part of each verse, a factual statement or observation of experience, conjures up the notion of the brevity of time. The remaining six syllables in each line project the poet's wishful prolongation of time through recollection:

> J'aime à vous voir en vos cadres ovales,
> Portraits jaunis des belles du vieux temps,
> Tenant en main des roses un peu pâles,
> Comme il convient à des fleurs de cent ans.
>
> . . . .
>
> Il est passé le doux règne des belles;
> La   Parabère   avec   la   Pompadour
> Ne trouveraient que des sujets rebelles,
> Et sous leur tombe est enterré l'amour.
>
> Vous, cependant, vieux portraits qu'on oublie,
> Vous respirez vos bouquets sans parfums,
> Et souriez avec mélancolie
> Au souvenir de vos gallants défunts.

["I like to see you in your faded egg-shaped frames, beautiful ladies of a bygone era, holding in your hands the slightly pale roses that somehow seem appropriate for flowers that are one hundred years old. . . . The genteel reign of the beautiful women has passed; the countess of Parabère and Madame de Pompadour would only find rebellious subjects now, and love has been buried with them in their graves. Nevertheless, old forgotten portraits, you still breathe the unscented flowers, and your sad smile recalls the memory of your deceased elegant ladies."]

The first stanza establishes such a delicately contrived balance between the past and the present that the reader is prepared to overlook or dismiss the awkward rhyme scheme in lines two and four, *ovales–pales*. The poet's melancholia is effectively counterpointed by the very portraits that he is contemplating. Gautier prevents his evocation from dwindling to another overbearing emotional statement on the inevitable fugacity of time in his last stanza when he alludes to the reconciliatory function of art. Thus, the sadness emanating from the three preceeding strophes is attenuated somewhat by the consolation that art records and preserves human experience that succumbs to time and space.

The frequently uncontrolled language and the quasi-hysterical manner in which Gautier elucidated the theme of "Pastel" in the 1838 edition of *La Comédie de la mort* underscored the fact that he had not succeeded definitively in resolving the conflict between objectivity and subjectivity in his aesthetic of Art for Art's Sake. The idea that death inevitably reduces to nothingness all human aspirations could hardly be considered an innovative theme in French Romanticism and in Gautier's poetic production for that matter. The poet casts *La Comédie de la mort* in the form of a semidramatic allegory, with man's foremost aspirations, love, knowledge, and personal glory, embodied in the respective fictional and historical personalities of Don Juan, Doctor Faustus, and Napoleon.

Two long narrative sections, somewhat pretentiously entitled, "La Vie dans la mort" [Life within death] and "La Mort dans la vie" [Death within life], serve as undisguised vehicles for the purely emotional conveyance of Gautier's obsessive fear of death. The ensuing monologues by the three figures comment gloomily on the futility attendant in all forms of human endeavor. The heavy hand of the poet's direction invests the various speeches with the kind of single-mindedness that eventually renders the monologues monotonous. The concluding strophe of *La Comédie de la mort* conveys the frenzied atmosphere that permeates the entire poem:

> *Mais quelle est cette femme*
> *Si pâle sous son voile? Ah! C'est toi, vieille infâme!*
> *Je vois ton crâne ras;*
> *Je vois tes grands yeux, prostituée immonde,*
> *Courtisane éternelle environnant le monde*
> *Avec tes maigres bras!*

["But, who is this woman who looks so pale under her veil? Oh! It's you, contemptuous old wretch! I can see your gaping eyes, vile prostitute; you are a perpetual courtesan embracing the world with your meagre arms!"]

While it remains undeniable that Gautier would seek to check such emotional outbursts in his future writing by an increased preoccupation with the facts revealed in external reality, it would be a gross simplification to assume that his aesthetic attitude was reduced to an exclusive concern with the artistic representation of the world of fact. To say with Gustave Lanson, for example, that Gautier's poetry after 1851 encourages purely visual responses to the virtual exclusion of any emotional reaction[5] is to strip *Emaux et camées* of much of its complexity, and to reduce the individual poems to a series of exercises in verbal portraiture.

The integration of the conception of plasticity into the aesthetic attitude of Art for Art's Sake constituted for Gautier the most convincing method by which he could arrive at giving permanent meaning to life which was by nature transitory. The cult of beauty to which he subscribed was based on the affirmation of the visible rather than the invisible world. If he sought to associate painting and sculpture with poetry, it was primarily because he believed that their concretized texture could endow the poet's words with the same hard and durable material. The identification which he sought to establish between sculpture and poetry rested more on an analogy than on any very convincing fact, and it was doubtless inspired by his personal philosophical outlook.

To be sure, there would be many instances in *Emaux et camées* where his poems would emerge as veritable word paintings of miniature objects. Yet such evocative portraits frequently manage to convey a particular vision or conception of the world which, through implication at least, appears to transcend the physical reality that is portrayed. As such, poems like "Affinités secrètes, mardigal panthéiste," "Le Château des souvenirs" [Remembered castles], and "Contralto," to mention by the most obvious, point more to the future development of Symbolism than to the adherence to rigid requirements of Art for Art's Sake. The sonnet, "L'Impassible" [The impassive one], which Gautier wrote in 1866, is a verbal celebration of the type of formal perfection which ultimately transcends the durability of the pure marble of the statue: "L'Infini s'est fondu dans vos larges prunelles, Et devant ce miroir qui ne réfléchit rien, L'Amour découragé s'asseoit, fermant ses ailes." ["Infinity dissolved in your large pupils, and before this mirror which does not reflect anything, the discouraged figure of Love sits, and closes its wings."] It is permitted to decipher in the rigidly controlled forms and the reduced material contours of poetry and sculpture the masked idealizations of the artists in question.

The formulation of the descriptive aesthetic of Art for Art's Sake and even Parnassianism resulted originally from Gautier's early yet fairly sustained attempt to dominate his intuitive attraction for the mysterious and the unknown. Despite his predisposition to the contrary, he rejected mysticism in favor of a more readily discernible plastic interpretation of reality in even the poems which are invested with unreal or fantastic backgrounds. For the most part, Gautier makes a conscious effort to achieve ironic detachment and plausibility.

The most satisfactory explanation of the nature of his artistic dilemma is voiced by his fictional counterpart in *Mademoiselle de Maupin*. D'Albert, the painter-poet confesses: ". . . the simple and natural side of things only comes to me after everything else, and I tend to grasp, first of all, that which is eccentric and bizarre." In terms that doubtless echo Gautier's personal reaction, he continues: "Through some instinctive compulsion, I have always desperately stuck to material objects, to the exterior silhouette of things, and I have given a very prominent place to plasticity in art." [6] The essentially plastic presentation of beauty constitutes one of the dominant motifs discernible in Gautier's literary production especially during the 1840s and 1850s.

In the main, the proponents of Art for Art's Sake sought to convey their perceptions of what appeared to be enduring examples of external beauty in descriptive language that alluded directly to concrete reality. It may be said that the most ostensible aim in Gautier's fiction and poetry was the actual revelation of such beauty and physical loveliness. *Mademoiselle de Maupin*, *La Toison d'or*, and *La Chaîne d'or* [The golden chain], most notably, have plots that evolve around the problem of of concealment and revelation of the beautiful.[7] The quest for idealized beauty, for the most part enjoined to the poet or fictional protagonist's conception of love, tends to become complicated by a more spiritual or transcendental quality after the mid-1850s.

Such narratives as *Jettatura* (1856) and *Spirite* (1865) as well as a significant number of poems in the *Poésies inédites et poésies posthumes* [Unedited and posthumous poems] refer with increasing frequency to ideals that prove accessible only through the imagination.[8] As such, these poems and stories represent a movement away from the earlier and more exclusively materialistic interpretations still much in evidence in many of the pieces of *Emaux et camées*. *Spirite*, for example, underscores a negative reaction to Gautier's initial conception of Art for Art's Sake and plasticity. Lavinia, the fictional glorification of perfect beauty, confesses that she has come to know her lover, the solitary poet, Guy de Malivert, through the poems he has written. What Lavinia explicates concerning the nature of art contributes significantly to our understanding of Gautier's aesthetic code:

> What authors actually say should not always be taken literally. One should always make concessions to the philosophical or aesthetic code, to the current affectations in vogue, to the required reticence for good taste, to the style that is desired, in short, to all that which can modify the writer's external presentation. But the perceptive reader can always decipher the author's underlying attitude under all these disguises. The poet's innermost thoughts may be frequently detected between the lines, and the secret which he means to keep from the great public may be surmised along the way as one by one the veiled enigmas contained behind each word are revealed.[9]

As we have already stated, the implicit conflict between material and spiritual forces in Gautier's own philosophical views eventually asserted itself in a manner so as to enhance his lyrical expression to a significant degree. The relationship between the plastic atmosphere of his descriptions and the emotional attitude that made itself manifest frequently endows his poems with an almost dramatic tension. Gautier voices his own predicament with characteristic irony when he describes Tiburce's choice in *La Toison d'or*: "If he could not smell the sweetness of the perfume, he would concentrate on the elegance of its vase." The fourth sonnet, "La vraie esthétique" [The real aesthetics], in the *Poésies inédites et poésies posthumes* stated the case more aptly with sensuous allusiveness:

Nous causions sur le beau, lui savant, moi poète;
Au galbe de l'amphore, il préférait le vin,
Il appelait le style, un grelot creux et vain,
Et la rime, un écho dont le sens s'inquiète.

Je répondais: 'La forme, aux yeux donne une fête!
Qu'il soit plein de Falerne ou d'eau prise au ravin,
Qu'importe! si le verre a le profil divin!
Le parfum envolé, reste la cassolette.'

Vous écoutiez, rêveuse, et mon oeil voyageant
Pendant que je cherchais un argument quelconque,
Suivait, sur les coussins, vos beaux pieds s'allongeant.

Tels les pieds de Vénus au rebord de sa conque,
Une écume de plis caressait leur contour,
Et semblait murmurer: Le vrai beau, c'est l'amour!

["We were discussing beauty, he, a scholar, and myself, a poet. He preferred the wine to the well-shaped contours of the vase. He called style an empty and vacuous bell, and rhyme, for him, was but an echo that only served to confuse meaning. I answered him: 'Beautiful forms provide a feast for the eyes! What does it matter whether it be filled with the perfumed wine of Falerno or with water drawn from a ravine, as long as the container possesses perfect contours! If the volatile scent escapes, there always remains the elegant vase.' While you were dreamily listening and I was searching for explanations, my eyes caught sight of the cushions that meandered around your beautiful outstretched feet. They were like those of Venus at the edge of the water shell whose lovely shape was caressed by a foam of folds which seemed to whisper: true beauty is love."]

By emphasizing the plastic beauty which his senses may perceive, Gautier avoids the risks and dangers inherent in the projection of more purely speculative interpretations of reality. The representation of the evident material aspects of the beautiful provided him with the most practical means of satisfying his urgent need to create beauty.

Reworked and augmented no less than six times from the initial appearance of its eighteen poems in 1852 to the forty-seven pieces contained in the definitive edition of 1872, *Emaux et camées* exercised a continuing influence on the poets of the French Parnassian movement until the advent of the Third Republic. Gautier's collection, the affirmation of his ideal of external beauty, proved to be as noteworthy for its aesthetic intention as for its actual artistic success. The title, *Emaux et camées*, conveyed the poet's resolve to consider each of the poems as individually polished works of art: enamels are miniatures that require delicate manipulation, and cameos are precious stones whose beauty may be further enhanced by elegantly sculptured shapes and contours.

Like the bejewelled objects alluded to in the title, *Emaux et camées* asserted the triumph of artistic effort over the stubbornly resistant materials found in external reality. The octosyllabic verse structure of the overwhelming majority of poems contained in *Emaux et camées* provided Gautier with a uniform mold to suit the variegated subject matter of his inspiration. The narrowness of the octosyllabic line suggests the poet's painstaking effort to give shape and cohesiveness to his ideas. The idea of miniature jewels is so well related to the eight-syllable line that it bequeathes *Emaux et camées* an artistic as well as formal unity. Moreover, Gautier's renovated use of the familiar sixteenth-century form with its workmanlike precise rhythms and carefully devised rhyme scheme constituted a welcome reform of French versification which had suffered from neglect at the hands of the majority of Romantic poets.[10]

If Gautier suggests an artistic affinity with poetry in his manifesto poem, "L'Art," it is more evidently established with sculpture than with painting. In his eloquent plea for the need of formal discipline in lyricism, he alludes explicitly to the painstaking procedure of the sculptor:

> *Point de contraintes fausses!*
> *Mais que pour marcher droit*

> *Tu chausses,*
> *Muse, un cothurne étroit.*
>
> . . . .
>
> *Lutte avec le carrare,*
> *Avec le paros dur*
> > *Et rare,*
> *Gardiens du contour pur.*
>
> . . . .
>
> *Sculpte, lime, cisèle;*
> *Que ton rêve flottant*
> > *Se scelle*
> *Dans le bloc résistant!*

["Avoid all useless hindrances! In order to walk straight, Muse, put on a slender buskin. . . . Struggle with the Carrara marble, and with the hard, rare Parian stone, guardians of the pure contour. . . . Carve, file, chisel; and may your vague inspiration be sealed in the hard, resistant rock."]

Gautier's insistent reference to the art of the sculptor in his poem is doubtless motivated by his desire to endow lyricism with a greater consciousness of form and structure. The poet's preoccupation with formal aspects will prevent him from indulging in the kind of reckless expansiveness that leaves the imagination unchecked. Many critics of *Emaux et camées* have allowed themselves to become overly influenced by Gautier's stated identification between poetry and sculpture in "L'Art," with the consequent effect that their individual assessments of the poems, for the most part, betray a far greater concern with the detection of the technical and descriptive applications of his thesis than of the lyrical ingredients that are unquestionably present.

It is no exaggeration to state that the literalism of sculpture as an art strikes us much less suited to the conveyance of the hidden powers inherent in lyrical expression than painting or music, for example. To say with so many critics [11] that the poetry in *Emaux et camées* merely reproduces the coldness and aloofness of marble statuary at the expense of any real conviction is to reduce Gautier's collection to a series of experimental exercises in so-called objective and descriptive verse. Pierre Michel has stated the case with greater accuracy when he described the *Emaux et camées* as the end product of the poet's intimate affinity with the techniques of the painter rather than those of the sculptor.[12]

To be sure, there exist in the *Emaux et camées* a considerable number of poems which correspond at least partially if not completely to the spirit of the tenets propounded in Gautier's program poem. The enamels and cameos referred to in the title receive their fullest justification in such tightly constructed poems as "Etude de mains" [Study on hands], "Symphonie en blanc majeur" [Symphony in white major], "La Montre" [The watch], "Les Néréides" [The sea nymphs] and "La Rose thé" [The tea rose], to mention but the most prominent. But there are in juxtaposition an important number of poems, such as "Bûchers et tombeaux" [Funeral pyres and tombs] and "Le Château du souvenir" [The castle of recollection] which project a sense of melancholia more immediately associated with the impassioned lyricism of Romanticism than with the plastic objectives alluded to in "L'Art."

For all their outer reserve and discretion, many poems in Gautier's collection lay bare the type of sensitivity which saves them from emerging as static encrustations of the poet's observations of reality. There is frequently present in the *Emaux et camées* an effective pictorial quality which enables the imagination to take flight from the all too recognizable world of contingencies into an idealized realm. The fact of the matter is that many of Gautier's verses emerge as veritable word paintings whose suggestiveness prolongs in the mind the image that is conveyed by a highly descriptive language. The opening poem of the collection, "Affinités secrètes: madrigal panthéiste," first published in the 15 January 1849 edition of the *Revue des Deux Mondes*, alludes thematically to an intuitive feeling shared with other poets such as Nerval, Hugo, and Baudelaire. "Affinités secrètes" takes up technically where the first sonnet in *Poésies* left off. More than a schematic and precious compilation,[13] "Affinités secrètes" sets the tone and conveys the depth of the poet's artistic aspirations in the collection.

To join the idea of ideal beauty with predestination, Gautier makes clever use of the madrigal form in which the poet ostensibly addresses his overtures to an unnamed lady, the physical embodiment of love and beauty. In a collection like *Emaux et camées*, the very title of "madrigal panthéiste" constitutes a playfully malicious allusion to the ambiguous character of that which will follow. The poem is an admirable illustration of Gautier's formal dominance over subject matter.

"Affinités secrètes" announces an important theme which the reader would expect to see treated in a grandiose manner. The reduced formal metres to which Gautier has recourse shows to which extent he has been able to dominate the personal impulse of his inspiration. As such, the poem underscores the dramatic improvement which he has achieved over his initial attempt to poeticize the same subject in the first sonnet of *Poésies*. The slight, delicate rhythms emerge so subtly from the octosyllabic lines that they endow the harsh juxtaposition made between the resistant blocks of outer reality and the white vaporous dreams of the mind with an unusual sense of calmness and repose. The idea of the eternal transformation of beings which takes place in the crucible of nature before the final renascence in other shapes and forms is effectively suggested through the graduating evocations of the marble, the pearl, the rose, the dove, and finally the lovers. Gautier isolates each of the elements found in the real world from their actual context so as to reassemble and unite them in the more ideal world of the poetic mind. The suggestion of the possible relationship between the various elements of the sensual world enjoins the reader to delve further than the immediate world of fact, appearance and hard contours in order to obtain the desired unity between mind and matter.

The last four stanzas of "Affinités secrètes" suggest the alternation of the theme of individual existence with that of universal identification:

> L'amour oublié se réveille,
> Le passé vaguement renaît,
> La fleur sur la bouche vermeille
> Se respire et se reconnaît.
>
> Dans la nacre où le rire brille,
> La perle revoit sa blancheur;
> Sur une peau de jeune fille,
> Le marbre ému sent sa fraîcheur.
>
> Le ramier trouve une voix douce,
> Echo de son gémissement,
> Toute résistance s'émousse,
> Et l'inconnu devient l'amant.
>
> Vous devant qui je brûle et tremble,
> Quel flot, quel fronton, quel rosier,
> Quel dôme nous connut ensemble,
> Perle ou marbre, fleur ou ramier?

["Forgotten love reawakens and the past is vaguely reborn; one remembers and inhales the perfume of the flower on the ruby lips. The pearl recognizes its own whiteness in the bright laughter of the lustre of beads, and the marble is visibly moved as it smells its own coolness on the skin of some maiden. The ringdove acknowledges in its soft call the echo of its own lament, and all resistance is blunted as the unknown person becomes the lover. You, for whom I pine and before whom I tremble, do you know which wave, which ornamental facade, which rose tree or which dome it was that knew us together as pearl or marble, flower or ringdove?"]

There exist fewer better examples of Gautier's successful externalization of his inner feeling than the

"Affinités secrètes." The poem is an idealized interpretation of the chain of being, an hypothesis frequently invoked in the poetry of the French Romanticists. The poem displays the poet's complete mastery over his emotions as it quietly unfolds the transformation of inanimate matter to higher human forms. The allusion to marble in the opening stanzas evokes the splendor of the ancient Greek temples, and the reference to the pearl, bedded at the bottom of the sea, translates the bejewelled conversion of the marble that had fallen into ruin. The roses in the gardens of the Alhambra and the two ringdoves that are lodged on the dome of Saint Mark are Gautier's obvious attempts at idealization, and they lead smoothly to the concluding affirmation of harmony, beauty, and love. "Affinités secrètes" crystallizes into a remarkably well contained statement the poet's desire to invest outer and inner reality with a unifying material principle. On this level, at least, it anticipates the synesthesia of Baudelaire's "Harmonies du soir" [evening harmony].

Gautier's well-known enthusiasm for what he considered decadent literature, articulated in his "Notice" to the 1868 edition of *Les Fleurs du Mal*, stemmed from his love of the artificial and his hatred of the useful and the modern. For the most part, his poetry was characterized by a somewhat paradoxical rejection of modernity and a forceful endorsement of the artistic refinement achieved by ancient and modern civilizations.[14]

If nothing else, *Émaux et camées* exposes the poet's marked predilection for pagan Antiquity: many of the pieces may be taken as spirited hymns of praise to the classical ideal and temperament. Antiquity's remoteness from the crass considerations of the present corresponded most closely with an aesthetic founded on autonomy and the idealization of external beauty. By contrast, the gothic and the grotesque, evident byproducts of Christianity, unveiled an obvious moral preoccupation by its insistent stress on the horrible aspects of existence and the inevitability of death. Beneath the surface veneer of "Bûchers et tombeaux," the poet's melancholic disenchantment with contemporary Christianity may be detected in verses that alternate with words of tribute to pagan Antiquity.

In a sense, the poem underscores the clash between the classical and Christian attitudes, and discloses Gautier's preference for the former:

> Des dieux que l'art toujours révère
> Trônaient au ciel marmoréen;
> Mais l'Olympe cède au Calvaire,
> Jupiter au Nazaréen;
>
> Une voix dit: Pan est mort!—L'ombre
> S'étend.—Comme sur un drap noir,
> Sur la tristesse immense et sombre
> Le blanc squelette se fait voir.
>
> .   .   .   .
>
> Reviens, reviens, bel art antique,
> De ton paros étincelant
> Couvrir ce squelette gothique;
> Dévore-le, bûcher brûlant!

["The gods, which the arts always revered, reigned under the Marmorian skies; but Olympus made way for Calvary, and Jupiter submitted to the Nazarene. A voice cried out: Pan is dead! The shadows spread out. The white skeleton figure appeared as if against a funereal sheet in an atmosphere heavy with gloom and sadness. Return, return, beautiful art of Antiquity, and cover this gothic skeleton with your Parian marble. Consume the skeleton, burning funeral pyre!"]

For all his outward concern with objectivity and impassibility, Gautier cannot refrain from frequent indirect allusions to the nature of his own egocentric predicament. The theme of the hermaphrodite in "Contralto" takes up where *Mademoiselle de Maupin* left off in exposing the poet's quasi-Platonic quest for absolute beauty. First published in the 15 December 1849 issue

of *La Revue des Deux Mondes,* "Contralto" amplifies
the thesis advanced in the earlier novel that the modern
idealization of woman assumes the function and position of the mythical Adonis and Hermaphrodite:
". . . you are the worthy representative of the first di-
vinity on earth, the purest symbol of the eternal essence:
beauty." [15] There is a decidedly Platonic strain in Gautier's ready identification of matter and essence, and in
his idolization of beauty that is the personification of
divine thought and inspiration. With Plato, Gautier
looked upon woman as a guide leading to an ideal; unlike the Greek philosopher, however, who considered
love as a means to rise in contemplation of divine
beauty, Gautier made of his love for idealized beauty
the object of his quest. "Contralto" makes vivid use of
the Pygmalion motif: the statue comes to life and emits
sounds that evoke the voiced aspirations of ideal lovers
of the past.

By his obvious response to inner experience, Gautier
reveals an essentially Romantic trait, but as Georges
Poulet points out, he refrains ultimately from utilizing
his consciousness to turn in upon himself. Gautier's
tendency is to turn himself outward. [16] "Contralto" remains the poet's most forceful statement on the fulness
of love and beauty.

> *Chimère ardente, effort suprême*
> *De l'art et de la volupté,*
> *Monstre charmant, comme je t'aime*
> *Avec ta multiple beauté!*
>
> .   .   .   .
>
> *Rêve de poète et d'artiste,*
> *Tu m'as bien des nuits occupé,*
> *Et mon caprice qui persiste*
> *Ne convient pas qu'il s'est trompé.*
>
> *Mais seulement il se transpose,*
> *Et, passant de la forme au son,*

Trouve dans sa métamorphose
La jeune fille et le garçon.

Que tu me plais, ô timbre étrange!
Son double, homme et femme à la fois,
Contralto, bizarre mélange,
Hermaphrodite de la voix!

["Burning chimera and supreme achievement of art and sensual delight, how I love you, charming monster, in your multiple beauty! . . . You are the dream of every poet and artist. I have been kept awake many nights attempting to obtain your multiplicity because there is in me a stubborn impulse that refuses to concede that it is impossible to realize. Instead I only transpose and transform form into sound, and thus I find in this kind of metamorphosis an expression of the ideal boy and girl. How I enjoy hearing the strange sound of your voice! It suggests man and woman together and at once. Contralto, you are an unusual mixture, the hermaphrodite of the human voice!"]

Along with such poems as "Coquetterie posthume" [The posthumous flirtation] and "Le Monde est méchant" [The world is evil], "Ce que disent les hirondelles" [What the swallows are saying] constitutes one of the best illustrations of Gautier's artistic achievement in *Emaux et camées*. Self-dubbed as "the man who believed in the reality of the external world," Gautier often excelled in producing poems that resulted from the artful collaboration of his personal observations with his poetic imagination. In their attempt to conceal personal emotion, the *Emaux et camées*, for the most part, reveal rather explicitly that which the poet has seen and that which he has imagined. It is usually through implication that one ventures to decipher his personal thoughts and feelings. In an obvious reaction to the Romantic outbursts and effusiveness of so many of his contemporaries, he made every effort to disassociate his own feelings from the external contexts to which he alluded in his verse. This should not be construed to mean, however, that he sought to silence the expression of his aspirations. His aesthetic ideal, for example, receives prominent mention not only in the *Emaux et camées*, so eagerly associated with Art for Art's Sake, but in his other prose and poetry as well.

"Ce que disent les hirondelles" communicates the poet's personal vision in language that has been exteriorized through visual references and the use of highly evocative local color. Gautier's personal aspiration is mentally associated with the physical flight of the swallows toward sunnier climates. The possibility of the theme's triteness and banality is much reduced by the technical skill with which the entire poem has been handled. The avoidance of any specific thematic allusion until the two concluding stanzas prevents the poem from degenerating into embarrassing pretentiousness. The "wings! wings! wings!" of stanza sixteen, for example, however banal or high flown it may strike us, does not enter into any greater personal elaboration than "to be able to fly with them [the swallows] toward the golden sun and the green springtime!"

What Gautier has managed to achieve in "Ce que disent les hirondelles" is a pleasing contrast between the workings of his own fanciful imagination and the visual effectiveness of the various tableaus and sketches. The chatter of the individual swallows evokes splendid visions of color and light through the descriptive allusions to such places as Athens, Rhodes, Malta, and Egypt. The accompanying factual indications blend neatly into each brief monologue. What emerges from the poem is an exquisite and elegant autumnal portrait that is clearly more notable for its charm than for its thematic profundity. The speeches of the fifth and sixth swallows convey the sense of the picturesque which punctuates "Ce que disent les hirondelles."

> La cinquième: "Je ferai halte,
> Car l'âge m'alourdit un peu,
> Aux blanches terrasses de Malte,
> Entre l'eau bleue et le ciel bleu."

La sixième: "Qu'on est à l'aise
Au Caire, en haut des minarets!
J'empâte un ornement de glaise,
Et mes quartiers d'hiver sont prêts."

["The fifth one says: 'Because of my declining years, I
shall stop on the white terraced banks of Malta between
the blueness of the sea and the skies.' The sixth one
counters: 'How comfortable one can feel in Cairo,
lodged on the top of some minaret! I merely paste together an ornament from the clay, and my winter
quarters are ready.' "]

Théophile Gautier's influence on the Parnassian poets
during the 1850s and 1860s was undeniably significant.
His works, tempered by a fairly sustained caution and
restraint, attempted to place style at the service of ideas
through the projection of imagery that readily associated
itself with the recognizable world of fact and external
experience. By and large, his verse translates a conscious
concern with lucidity that is aimed at clarifying rela-
tively plain emotions and relationships. The restraint
that accompanied his poetic impulse may have prevented him, at times, from achieving and sustaining the
kind of intensity that invests great lyrical expression.

Gautier's genius and limitation as a poet have been
appraised by no less distinguished literary figures than
Baudelaire and Huysmans. The former expressed his
unbridled enthusiasm for the author of *Emaux et
camées* in the dedicatory statement of *Les Fleurs du
Mal*: "For the truly impeccable poet, the perfect ma-
gician of French letters, for my dear and venerated
master and friend, Théophile Gautier, I dedicate these
sickly flowers as an expression of my profound esteem."
Through his fictional protagonist, Des Esseintes, Huysmans paid Gautier tribute that was couched in reservation: "Similarly, after cherishing him for many years,
Des Esseintes was beginning to lose interest in Gautier's
work; his admiration for the incomparable painter of
word-pictures that Gautier was had recently been di-

minishing day by day, so that now he was more as-tonished than delighted by his almost apathetic descriptions." [17] The modern reader of Gautier's verse is apt to situate his critical judgment somewhere between Baudelaire's unabashed praise and Huysmans's polite reservations.

3

Théodore de Banville and the Obsession with Formal Perfection

The fact that so many critics and literary historians continue to identify Théodore de Banville as the author of the "official" exposition of Parnassian doctrine constitutes one of the most singular ironies that has sprung from the history of the movement. When *Le Petit Traité de poésie française* first appeared as serialized chapters in the *Echo de la Sorbonne* in 1870, it provoked the immediate displeasure of Leconte de Lisle and the more prominent practitioners of Parnassianism.

For all of its obvious concern with rhyme and rhythm and the technical intricacies of French versification, Banville's treatise conveyed a disturbingly cavalier approach to the problem of poetic expression which only served to irritate his more serious and staid congeners. The very desultoriness of his half-serious, half-ironic remarks on form and inspiration invested his essay with precisely the kind of debonair attitude that appeared to undermine the seriousness of the problem at hand.[1] The fact of the matter was that *Le Petit Traité de poésie française*, as a Parnassian statement on the art of versification, rested upon a most ironic if not altogether grotesque paradox.

Banville interspersed his commentary with such frequent reference to the genius of Hugo that *Le Petit Traité* reads, at various intervals, as an eloquent homage to the illustrious poet of the French Romantic movement. Moreover, the generous acknowledgment made to Hugo, Tennint, and Sainte-Beuve in the sections on rhyme, meter and rhythm virtually endowed the treatise with a distinctly partisan Romantic ingredient. With the exception of Glatigny, the Parnassian poets dismissed Banville's attempt to formalize the rules of poetic expression as an inept if not unfortunate pleasantry. Banville's curious admiration for Hugo's lyricism, as a practicing Parnassian, sprang from the contradictory impulses he felt within himself as a poet. His ostensible adherence to Parnassian doctrine from 1866 to 1886 was motivated principally by his determination to dominate his inspiration so that it might be enclosed in forms that would best ensure its survival in art. The Parnassian conception of artistic permanence, suggested through the hard and plastic texture of carefully contrived forms and imagery, appealed to him sufficiently to make of him a champion of Art for Art's Sake despite his professional esteem for the poetry of Victor Hugo.

In actual fact, *Le Petit Traité de poésie française* lacks the kind of scholarly and scientific rigor that would have enlisted the enthusiasm and approbation of Leconte de Lisle and Heredia. The treatise's real value lies in that which it reveals about Banville's poetic philosophy. It has been convincingly illustrated that his intransigent theoretical stand on rhyme and meter and his categorical rejection of enjambment and inversion, for example, are repeatedly and somewhat shamelessly contradicted in his own poetic practice.[2] What *Le Petit Traité* unveils is the poet's enervated attempt to camouflage personal poetic inspiration with the kind of external formal accouterment that would impart his verse with a greater sense of objectivity and impassibility. It is precisely the detectable unfolding of Banville's quest for formal perfection in order to conceal his essentially Romantic temperament that infuses his verse, from time to time, with a decipherable lyrical quiver.

Banville's psychological attachment to the spirit of Romanticism asserted itself with startling effrontery in the 1871 edition of Lemerre's *Parnasse contemporain*.

The "Ballade de ses regrets pour l'an 1830" [Ballad on his nostalgia for the year 1830], composed in 1869, underscored the poet's obvious preference for the expansive lyricism associated with Hugo and Musset. Banville's nostalgic recollection of the opening of the July Monarchy contrasts the more hopefully expectant mood of the era with the overriding disillusionment and pessimism that characterized Parnassian expression during the 1860s. The "Ballade de ses regrets" identified Banville spiritually with the bygone Romanticism of the 1830s in the official publication of the Parnassian poets:

> O Poésie, ô ma mère mourante,
> Comme tes fils t'aimaient d'un grand amour,
> Dans ce Paris, en l'an mil huit cent trente.
> Enfant divin, plus beau que Richelieu,
> Musset chantait; Hugo tenait la lyre,
> Jeune, superbe, écouté comme un dieu.
> Mais à présent, c'est bien fini de rire.

["Oh Poetry! my dying mother, know how your sons loved you in Paris during the year 1830! Musset, the enchanting child, much more handsome than Richelieu, sang your hymn. The young and splendid Hugo played on his lyre, and the people listened to him as if he were a god. But now, the time is gone for hope and laughter."]

Le Petit Traité de poésie française, to a degree, corroborated Banville's sense of nostalgia for the past. His insistent recommendation that poets return to the use of such poetic forms as the rondeau, the triolet and the ballad, so popular during the Middle Ages and the Renaissance, was motivated principally by the desire to disassociate himself from the bleakness of the 1860s and 1870s. The rondeau, the triolet, and the ballad evoked the kind of grace, wit, and gaiety which Banville urgently sought to restore to his own verse and to that of his contemporaries.

To achieve the sense of remoteness from the present and to suggest the carefree fantasy which he associated with the poetic forms of the Middle Ages and the

Renaissance, Banville urged that painstaking care be given to the elaboration of a pleasing rhyme scheme in poetry. Indeed, the aphorism on the importance of rhyme in *Le Petit Traité* constituted the central point around which all other considerations converged: "Rhyme emerges as the only harmony achieved in verse, and rhyme makes up the entire verse." Banville's conception of the rhyme can hardly be considered as original; Sainte-Beuve enunciated the same principle earlier in his *Tableau historique et critique de la poésie française et du théâtre français au XVIe siècle* [Historical and critical survey of French poetry and theatre in the sixteenth century].

For Banville, harmony was the springboard that permitted the poet-clown to turn somersaults into the gayety and grace of the Middle Ages and the Renaissance. If he chose to render both ideas and inspiration subservient to rhyme, it was in order to achieve the type of harmony which he identified with art and poetry. In a sense, his advocacy of harmony in poetry pointed more in the direction of Symbolism than of Parnassianism. Moreover, his virtual obsession to obtain it stemmed from a Romantic urge to escape from his own predicament. His ostensible allegiance to Parnassianism was predicated upon the need to externalize the substance of his poetic inspiration into a workable mold and formula. Most of his verse translates such a visible preoccupation with rhyme and rhythm.

Three of Banville's best-known poetry collections, *Les Cariatides* (1842), *Les Stalactites* (1846), and *Améthystes* (1856) carry in their train strong intimations of durable substances and sharply defined contours in a manner reminiscent of Gautier's *Emaux et camées*. Indeed, it might be argued that each title indicated conveys a sense of remoteness and noninvolvement; like the jewels, enamels and semiprecious hangings, the individual poems are meant to appeal to the reader's visual imagination through the precision of their expression and the beauty of their imagery. The suggested alliance between poetry and sculpture, alluded to in Gautier's celebrated manifesto poem of 1857, "L'Art," was, to a certain degree, advanced by Banville a year earlier in the ode, "A Théophile Gautier." *Les Stalactites* of 1846, however, contained still another poem by Banville on the topic of plasticity and poetry.

This earlier poem is of interest to us because it reveals so well the frame of reference in which Banville approached the tenets of Art for Art's Sake and Parnassianism.

Sculpteur, cherche avec soin, en attendant l'extase,
Un marbre sans défaut pour en faire un beau vase;
Cherche longtemps sa forme et n'y retrace pas
D'amours mystérieux ni de divins combats;

. . . .

Qu'autour du vase pur, trop beau pour la Bacchante,
La verveine mêlée à des feuilles d'acanthe
Fleurisse, et que plus bas des vierges lentement
S'avancent deux à deux, d'un pas sûr et charmant,
Les bras pendant le long de leurs tuniques droites
Et les cheveux tressés sur leurs têtes étroites.

["Sculptor, while waiting for the ecstasy of inspiration, look carefully for a piece of flawless marble from which to make a beautiful vase. Think carefully before you decide on the shape you wish to give it, and do not try to portray on it the mysterious loves and the divine battles of mythology. . . . May the elegant contours of your perfect vase emerge too beautiful for the gaze of Bacchus's priestess, and let the ornamental verbenas, intertwined with the leaves of the acanthus, appear in full bloom. A little lower, show the slowly cadenced but charming procession of the virgins walking two by two, with their long slender arms gracefully drooping beside their straight tunics and with their hair braided on their narrow heads."]

Within the idealized context of Greek antiquity, Banville sought to define his conception of perfect, lasting beauty. The lines do not concern themselves with any actual fact or reality, but more precisely with a project involving the collaboration of two creative artists. What the poet conceives, the sculptor will attempt to render in a visibly durable work of art. What the poem reveals is Banville's rejection of any principle associated with violence or disorder. For all of its mosaic structure, the first part of the poem (only one line has been quoted in the excerpt) relates precisely what the artist should exclude from Greek mythology. The second part of this program poem appears in sharp antithesis to the first: the titanic battles of the demigods make way for the harmony and grace suggested in the images of the verbenas, the acanthus and the slow procession of the elegant virgins. The quasi-sculptural description of the virgins is endowed with a religious and distant purity which, in this instance, conforms perfectly to the Parnassian conception of objectivity and impassibility.

The technical dexterity, so prominently noticeable in this program piece, points to the development of Banville's remarkable talent for dealing with intricate rhymes and rhythms. The poem's directness proceeds from the conspicuous absence of any distracting type of inversion, and whatever enjambments may be detected serve to enhance and prolong the illusion of movement suggested by the mosaic tableaus and the sculptural portraits placed on the richly ornamented Greek vase. In a radical departure from sixteenth-century French versification, Banville arranges his *rimes riches* in alternating groups of two masculine rhymes and two feminine rhymes. The somewhat rapid pace of the beginning of the poem slows down progressively in the second part by a frequent recourse to words possessing more complicated rhythms and fuller sonorities: *lentement* and *charmant*, for example.

In short, the rhyme scheme employed conveys a detectable musical charm and reveals the conscious effort of the poet to obtain definite desired effects. This program poem, like the majority of those included in *Les Stalactites*, aims at the illustration of a simple and harmonious beauty rather than at the expression of any obvious sentiment or emotion. The ecstasy referred to in the opening line is that achieved through the quiet contemplation of a work of art. Such an ecstacy was expressly calculated to remove both the creative artist and the reader or the beholder from the immediate contingencies of a limited reality in order to transport them to an idealized world containing perfect forms and harmonies.

That Théodore de Banville's conception of Art for Art's Sake and Parnassianism stemmed from a predominant emphasis with the purely formal aspects of the aesthetic attitude is made readily evident by the manner in which he approached and interpreted Antiquity in his own verse. Maurice Souriau has called attention to the fact that Banville's conception of Greek antiquity was colored by an unconvincing attempt to reconcile pagan mythology with Christianity.[3] Indeed, Banville's own preface to "Sang dans la coupe" [Blood in the chalice] in the collection, *Les Cariatides*, lays bare his misreading of Louis Ménard's *Rêveries d'un païen mystique*: "Modern scholars on mythology such as Louis Ménard have illustrated that our Christian religion of love and forgiveness is in harmonious agreement with the Hellenic religions."

Banville's interpretation blatantly contradicts the thesis upheld by Ménard in his treatise. *Les Exilés* [The exiled gods] of 1867 purported to advance the idea that modern Christianity has forced the pagan deity of Antiquity into exile. All in all, the poems included in *Les Exilés* elicit a jarring and disconcerting effect by their indiscriminate intermingling of a sensual conception of paganism with a mystical view of Catholicism. The heroic scenes from "Le Forgeron" [The blacksmith] project a grotesquely inept attempt to wed Christianity to pagan mythology.

Insomuch as Banville sought to justify Antiquity before modern Christianity, he invested his verse with a disquieting if not exactly satisfying lyrical tremor. Anatole France has stated the case accurately: "The Venus of M. de Banville is a Venetian Venus. She does not at all resemble the Venus of mythology. She is rather, as painters say, a figure that flies at the ceiling. The Olympus of the poet is the Olympus one encounters in the banqueting-hall. Masquerading in carnival costumes, the cavaliers walk hand in hand with their ladies and dance gracefully under the adorned cupola to the sound of lifeless music. That is the kind of world M. Théodore de Banville evokes in his poetry." [4]

With discernible wryness, Banville frequently alluded to the fact that he sought to divest his verse of ideas, sentiments, and emotions that would prevent it from imparting a sense of playful or mindless abandonment. Most critics have been prepared to corroborate the poet's self-evaluation, and they link Banville's name with poetry that conveys a sense of formal perfection at the expense of any thematic profundity.

The preface to the collection, *Roses de Noël* [Christmas roses], published in 1878, reveals his propensity to comment on his poetic philosophy in terms that are subsequently contradicted by his own poetic practice. The dedicatory essay to his mother includes a defense of impassibility and pure art which states: "It is very rare that we show ourselves as good workmen when we write under the impulse of any genuinely felt sentiment or emotion." It is no small irony that one of the most effective pieces in *Roses de Noël*, "Querelle" [Quarrel] translates such an instance of real though perfectly controlled emotion. "Querelle" combines the poet's dream of formal precision with a delicate sense of personal intimacy. Both the rhyme and rhythm of the poem are ideally suited to the subject at hand: the family portrait of a mother with her two children on her knees.

Lorsque, ma soeur et moi, dans les forêts profondes,
Nous avions déchiré nos pieds sur les cailloux,
En nous baisant au front, tu nous appelais fous,
Après avoir maudit nos courses vagabondes.

Puis, comme un vent d'été confond les fraîches ondes
De deux petits ruisseaux sur un lit calme et doux,
Lorsque tu nous tenais tous deux sur tes genoux,
Tu mêlais en riant nos chevelures blondes.

Et pendant bien longtemps, nous restions là blottis,
Heureux, et tu nous disais parfois: 'O chers petits!
Un jour, vous serez grands, et moi je serai vieille'!

Les jours se sont enfuis d'un vol mystérieux,
Mais toujours la jeunesse éclatante et vermeille
Fleurit dans ton sourire et brille dans tes yeux.

["When my sister and myself bruised our feet on the
pebbles in the dark forest, you called us silly as you
kissed our foreheads after having accursed our wander-
lust. Then like a summer wind that intermingles the
fresh waves of two little brooks in the calm and gentle
riverbed, you intertwined our blond hair as you held us
on your knees. And we remained there for a long time
happily snuggled while you would say from time to
time: 'Oh, my dear little ones! You shall soon grow up
and I shall be an old woman!' The days fled like some
mysterious wind, but your brilliantly rosy youthfulness
still blooms in your smile and glitters in your eyes."]

The sonnet is striking for the soberness and for the
simplicity with which it depicts the exquisitely unassum-
ing portrait of the mother and the two children. The
two quatrains and the first tercet gently lead up to the
concluding tercet which is cast in the present tense and
forms a mild juxtaposition to the past tense utilized in
the rest of the poem. The formal aspects of "Querelle"
blend in perfect harmony with the scene that is projected. The rhythm of the first quatrain, jagged and
broken, conveys the excitement of the excursion into
the forest, while that of the second quatrain suggests the
smoothness and gentleness of the metaphor of a becalmed reality.

Banville cleverly invokes the tragic passage of time
with a slow yet deliberate rhythm in the first tercet that

is punctured by the mother's sigh in the first tercet. The sense of melancholia which penetrates the first line of the concluding tercet becomes significantly attenuated by the sonorously triumphant affirmation of the two last lines which celebrate the expression of lasting mental and spiritual youthfulness emanating from the radiant smile of the aging mother.

The entire sonnet is completely devoid of the kind of rash enjambments and jarring spurts which could have rhythmically clashed with the calm and peaceful resolution of "Querelle." Banville alludes to the inexplicably tragic passage of time as a mysterious flight; the expression is marvelously attuned to the preceding image of the children who will grow up and take flight on their own wings of maturity. The image of the flight of the bird extends itself virtually throughout the entire sonnet and lends it a decidedly delicate texture. The words, *blottis* and *chers petits* reinforce the expression *vol mystérieux* in the final tercet. The somewhat jagged and almost precipitous rhythm of the first quatrain endows the poem with just the right amount of dramatic intensity. "Querelle" illustrates one of the most successful unions achieved by formal and technical perfection and significant thematic treatment of a genuinely felt sentiment.

More frequently than not, however, Banville owes his reputation to the kind of cleverly devised *rondels* such as "La Lune" [The moon], for example, which mount slight thematic content into pleasantly contrived rhyme schemes. The following stanza illustrates his undeniable talent for construction of poetry, in this instance, from the alternation of two feminine rhymes:

> *Avec ses caprices, la Lune*
> *Est comme une frivole amante;*
> *Elle sourit et se lamente,*
> *Elle fuit et vous importune.*

["The moon, with its whims, is like a frivolous mistress: it smiles, then complains; it evades you, then it annoys

you."] "La Lune," scarcely more than a playful variation
on a rhyme scheme, corresponds more directly to the
spirit of the tenets elucidated in *Le Petit Traité de
poésie française* than does the more substantial
"Querelle."

Perhaps Banville's best-known poem, "Le Saut du
tremplin" [The somersault from the springboard], found
its way into the collection, *Odes funambulesques* [Fantastic
odes] which was published in 1857. "Le Saut du
tremplin" relates the mental triumph of the poet-clown
who seeks to emancipate himself from the crass contingencies
of an ugly and limited existence. Critics such
as René Lalou, for instance, have been eager to apply
the image to characterize summarily Banville's poetry.[5]
However banal the poem may strike us, it nevertheless
remains noteworthy as a technical tour de force. Banville's
clown resembles the Parnassian poet who attempts
to decipher an idealized beauty from the high summits
of contemplation. The idea of the insistent poetic effort
of the writer who wishes to escape into the idealized
realm of art and beauty is effectively conveyed by ascending
rhythms which accompany the energetic leaps of
the clown. Here is an instance in which rhythm constitutes
a prolongation of the image which is central to the
poem. Indeed, the rhythm provides a unifying rallying
point for what would have otherwise deteriorated into a
desultory program piece:

> "*Plus loin! plus haut! je vois encor*
> *Des boursiers à lunettes d'or,*
> *Des critiques, des demoiselles*
> *Et des réalistes en feu.*
> *Plus haut! plus loin! de l'air! du bleu!*
> *Des ailes! des ailes! des ailes!*"
>
> *Enfin de son vil échafaud,*
> *Le clown sauta si haut, si haut,*
> *Qu'il creva le plafond de toiles*
> *Au son du cor et du tambour,*
> *Et, le coeur dévoré d'amour,*
> *Alla rouler dans les étoiles.*

[" 'Farther! Higher! I can still see bankers in gold-rimmed eyeglasses, critics, spinsters and fiery pragmatists. Higher! Farther! Some air to breathe! The azure blue sky! Some wings! Some wings! Some wings!' Finally, at the accompanying sound of the horn and drum, the clown jumped so high from his wretched stand that he punctured the room's starred ceiling, and consumed with love, he went rolling among the stars."]

Viewed from Banville's own perspective and appreciated from a necessarily technical angle, the poems contained in such notable collections as *Les Cariatides*, *Les Stalactites*, and the *Odes funambulesques*, do convey a pleasing sense of wit, grace, and gayety. The evident narrowness of his poetic range limits, to an extent, the interest of the twentieth-century reader in Banville. Yet, the very lightweight quality of his verse provides the Parnassian movement with a sorely needed relief from more ponderous and scholarly considerations. It was perhaps Leconte de Lisle who described his poetry most accurately: ". . . he writes 'little' poems, but he is a poet, a poet endowed with a delicate instinct for all the shades of sound." [6] One might conclude that Banville was the *beau parleur* of the French Parnassian movement.

4

Leconte de Lisle and the
Historical Imagination

Leconte de Lisle's poetic idealization of past civilizations stemmed from a refusal to resolve the problems of his own predicament within the inherited contexts of nineteenth-century France. The personal disappointment and disenchantment which he suffered prior to 1848 crystallized into an abject sense of disillusionment after the proclamation of the Second Empire in 1851. With such notable literary congeners as Renan, Flaubert, and Baudelaire, Leconte de Lisle decried the regime of Louis-Napoleon for its blatant and cynical degeneracy, and he proceeded to contrast the moral, political, and artistic inferiority of French institutions with the glorious cultural attainments of ancient Greece and Rome.[1]

His own poetical contributions to the *Phalange* in the 1830s and 1840s betray a noticeable attempt to interpret mythology in a modern socialist framework, conspicuously aligned with the naïve Fourierist idealism of the journal. De Lisle's eventual spiritual defection from the society in which he lived sprang from a marked propensity to look back upon the past nostalgically rather than from any specific personal or ideological disillusionment he may have experienced.[2]

By 1848, his pessimistic stance with respect to the present and the future asserted itself bluntly and unmistakably in a letter dated 30 April 1848 to the noted Greek scholar, Louis Ménard: "What a filthy and disgusting brood humanity is! The people are so stupid:

They constitute a race doomed to perpetual slavery since they are unable to live without pack or yoke! . . . These masses that are so easy to deceive, may they croak from hunger and thirst! They will soon massacre their only real friends." De Lisle's professed hatred of the present led him logically to an idealization of the past through his creative imagination. But unlike the French Romantic poets who evolved highly intuitive explications of the human predicament, Leconte de Lisle sought deliberately to chasten his imaginative powers through the rigorous scrutiny and control of objective critical and scientific data. His consequent evocations of Greek art and civilization, for the most part, appear authenticated by historical study.

In the prefatory essay to the *Poèmes antiques* of 1852, de Lisle characterized much of his poetry as a series of documented studies or meditations on Antiquity. His virtual obsession with the past corresponded both to his love of plastic beauty and to the sense of disenchantment he felt with his own times. The preface to the *Poèmes antiques* and the subsequent *Discours de réception à l'Académie* [Address of acceptance to the academy] of 1886 underscore his objective to regenerate lyric expression, which in his estimation had fallen into a state of decadence, through an alliance with scholarship and scientific methodology.

What Leconte de Lisle actually meant by "science" has been aptly defined by Richard Chadbourne as a positive historical knowledge and especially that of past religious phenomena.[3] De Lisle's repeated recourse to the historical, religious, and legendary past in his lyric poetry stemmed from an enervating anticipation to discover the kind of unity and harmony that he found to be so conspicuously lacking in the nineteenth century. This detectable sense of anticipation invests much of his verse with the kind of lyric dimension that causes such epithets as "objective" and "impersonal" to appear almost superfluous. The fact of the matter was that de Lisle's advocacy that poetry be interlinked with science raised lyricism to the rank of a veritable religion or cult of beauty. Only when art shall have become sufficiently purified by science can the poet or the artist expect to resume meaningfully his awesome function as educator of humanity.

Leconte de Lisle's publication of six critical essays, *Les Poètes contemporains*, reaffirmed his decided preference for Antiquity over modernism. The preface to these studies constitutes a veritable rebuttal to the objections raised over the seeming untimeliness of most of his verse. His reply to the charge is as severe as it is haughty: "The true artist will never condescend to become a crowd pleaser: rather, he shuns what he knows to be a current vogue, and he invests his work with the most dispassionate kind of thought. He nourishes his poetry with sentiment that is both virile and discreet. True passion derives from art and not from sentimentality." [4]

Clearly, then, the nineteenth-century reader has significantly more to learn to appreciate from the examples of the glorious past than from the accomplishments of the ignominious present. Nor would de Lisle subscribe to Hugo and Vigny's handling of history and legend as mere vehicles in the exposition of attitudes that are essentially modern and topical. If the Romanticists made significant strides toward more plausible representation through their utilization of local color, their historical novels and dramas nevertheless lacked the stamp of authenticity derived only from the scholarly and methodical establishment of fact and locale. The successful literary evocation of the past is that one which enables the modern reader to understand the relationships that exist between individuals and their environments, between societies and their religious beliefs.

De Lisle distinguishes between the two possible aesthetic approaches to the past in his essay on Victor Hugo. He leaves no equivocation as to his preference.

One approach requires that the poet borrow from history or from legend merely the most suitable framework from which he may conveniently exploit the hopes and concerns of his own time. This is precisely what Victor Hugo accomplishes in *La Légende des siècles*. Contrarily, the other theory requires that the creative writer immerse himself completely in the period he has chosen to elucidate, and that he place himself mentally in the epoch that he wishes to recall.

Much of Leconte de Lisle's lyrical quality proceeds directly from the motivation that led him to pursue the past so unrelentingly. His four principal collections, *Les Poèmes antiques, Les Poèmes barbares, Les Poèmes tragiques,* and *Derniers poèmes* [Last poems] contain a significant number of poems which evoke the historical origins of man. In his disgust with his own times, he turned to Antiquity for the values he sought and which he found to be so sorely lacking in his own contemporary context.

If some of his verse in celebration of Greek idealism may strike us today as bordering on the panegyric, it is principally because of the poet's conviction that Antiquity alone succeeded in quenching man's thirst for ideal order, balance, and harmony. De Lisle's idealizations of ancient Greece and Rome, however, loom in sharp contrast with the classical literature of the French writers of the seventeenth century. The latter sought to adjust the spirit of Antiquity to the essentially Christian French temperament. De Lisle attempts to reverse the procedure by requesting that his readers adjust their nineteenth-century optic to the superior cultural values of the Ancients. Moreover, the verse in the *Poèmes antiques* and the *Poèmes barbares* differed significantly from the historical literary conceptions of the earlier French Romanticists. If Lamartine and Vigny considered the epic as a series of short yet closely interrelated philosophical poems which commented on the evolution of man's aspirations and achievements, they failed to exhaust the already-burgeoning historical studies which had appeared in their own time, and remained content to produce but fragmented visionary poems with *Jocelyn* and the *Poèmes antiques et modernes*.

What de Lisle advocated in his various prefaces and attempted in his own poetic practice was an assimilation of all the scholarly and scientific tendencies so prominently in evidence during the 1850s and 1860s. To restore to the poet his lost authority as teacher, de Lisle felt compelled to redefine the nature of poetry within the intellectual framework of positivist and scientific currents. While maintaining a visible aloofness from the pragmatic considerations of his time, the Parnassian poet would systematically study and explain the great laws and traditions of the past which served as actual bases for the institutions of the present. In de Lisle's view, the poet had a positive if not a practical service to render humanity: his poetic evocations of bygone civilizations underscored the human aspirations and the permanent values that ultimately united men of various races, creeds, and epochs. The authenticity of such historical poetry would be made to rest upon a thorough grounding not only in history but also in folklore, mythology, and in the recent philological exegeses of religious literature.

An important segment of Leconte de Lisle's verse recounts, in actual fact, the legendary history of religions. In his *Discours sur Victor Hugo* before the French Academy, he sharply criticized the author of *La Légende des siècles* [The legend of the centuries] for his purely subjective appraisal of religious experience in history. Religious sentiment occupies an important place in the poetic production of Leconte de Lisle because of a fundamental conviction that the various forms of religion have consistently sought to articulate and preserve the idealistic aspirations of men throughout the ages. If he emphasized the fact that no single religion possessed any justifiable claim to absolute truth, he held that each religious attitude projected elements of truth at specific times and places: "An illustrious writer once commented that man creates the notion of holiness out of that in which he believes as he creates the idea of beauty out of that which he loves."

De Lisle's religious views may hardly be termed original since they shared much in common with the ideas of Ménard and Renan on the matter. If de Lisle remained adamant in rejecting the Judeo-Christian explication of man's ultimate unity, he admitted with such literary historians as Benjamin Constant (*De la Religion,* 1824) and Edgar Quinet (*Le Génie des religions,* 1841) that religions and the myths they engender are valid because they tend to reveal at least partial elements of the divine. There can be little doubt that his own predilection for Greek antiquity is firmly rooted in his understanding and appreciation of polytheism as the religious creed best attuned to both the material and spiritual aspirations of man. The persistence and the conviction with which he attempts to illustrate the superiority of the idealism of ancient Greece infuses his best verse with an undeniable sense of lyrical intensity.

The question of Leconte de Lisle's erudition in his poems on Greek and Roman antiquity, such as it was posed by some of the best-known critics of the nineteenth and twentieth centuries, underlines the extent to which he frequently projected his personal interpretations upon his poetic evocations of the past. Among the earlier critics,[5] only Jean Psichari considered de Lisle's poems erudite and convincing recreations of Greek antiquity. Other literary historians such as Joseph Vianey have suggested that the poet had recourse to only the most general and summary documents, and that his *Poèmes antiques* more frequently than not translate his personal prejudices and dispositions.

Whether or not de Lisle had been sufficiently well tutored by Louis Ménard, France's most distinguished Hellenist during the second half of the century, has been clearly and definitively ascertained more recently by Irving Putter and Alison Fairlie.[6] Yet, the question raised by the critics carries in its train the more central issues of the poet's supposed objectivity and impersonality. The two terms, so frequently invoked with respect to Parnassian poetry in general and to Leconte de Lisle in particular, have unfortunately engendered more confusion than elucidation concerning the position of the poets of Art for Art's Sake. The concept of impassibility did not convey the idea that the poet would have to suppress all expression of his personality in his lyricism. As leader of the Parnassian poets, de Lisle advocated that the poet express his personality more discreetly and unobtrusively than some of their Romantic counterparts, such as Musset, for example. Richard Chadbourne has astutely observed that both Flaubert and Leconte de Lisle frequently referred to the terms as means invented to disguise their respective inner worlds so that only the perceptive reader might detect and discover them.[7] Surface objectivity and impersonality invest de Lisle's poetry with a discreet yet no less effective lyrical dimension.

In his appraisal of Leconte de Lisle's verse concerning past civilizations, Maurice Souriau reproaches the poet for contaminating his evocations of ancient Greece with a stark philosophy of personal absorption into nothingness. Souriau's reproach may serve as the poet's ironic exoneration of an earlier accusation that he callously turned his back on his own times. The interjection of personal views and prejudices constituted the only means by which the poet could contrast a past era with the present. Yet de Lisle has managed to camouflage skilfully his personal distress within an apparent attitude of objectivity and impersonality by the frequent erudition which he displays. The truth of the matter remains that when de Lisle blends his personal reactions into the elaborate landscape descriptions, the result achieved is nearly always felicitous. That the poet's illumination of the past may at times appear mannered is only predictable since, despite whatever else he may contend, the poet is compelled to convey a vision from his own optic if he is to achieve the lyrical effect he desires.

Pierre Flottes has aptly described de Lisle's poetry as "a cry of passion disguised in an historical allegory."[8]

Whether or not the poet reconstructs the history of religions in his verse from the vantage point of his disbelief proves irrelevant to the intrinsic effects he achieves in the individual poems. It matters little whether or not the poet has actually contemplated the statue of the Venus of Milo; the unalterable fact remains that the poem succeeds in conveying a sense of perfect beauty. If Leconte de Lisle encouraged his followers to camouflage their feelings and passions under a layer of objectivity and a cloak of erudition, he did not advocate that they stifle their imagination and their emotions. One may easily subscribe to Souriau's judgment: "His Greek poems are a festival, a veritable fairyland for the imagination."[9]

The thirty-one poems published initially in the 1852 edition of the *Poèmes antiques* contain the basic themes which Leconte de Lisle continued to develop until his death in 1894. The fact that the definitive edition of 1874 comprised some twenty-five additional pieces, derived essentially from the same sources of inspiration as the earlier poems, confirms the widely held assumption that his poetic and philosophical outlook remained fairly consistent after 1848.

As the title of the collection suggests, the majority of the *Poèmes antiques* celebrate the poet's conception of an idealized plastic beauty which he had found to exist in Greek civilization. The inclusion of such poems as "Hélène," "Niobé," and "La Vénus de Milo," previously published in the *Phalange* as lyrical prefigurations of the Fourierist doctrine of earthly harmony, points to the considerable change in attitude undergone by the poet as a result of the political fiascos of 1848 and 1851. Now pruned of their political idealism, the poems join the other Greek poems as expressions of materialist beauty rendered permanent by the artistic efforts of sculptors, painters, and poets. Yet, the tone and the mood of the volume hardly permit the *Poèmes antiques* to be catalogued as joyous or exalted lyricism. The poet's metaphysical pessimism, derived from both his personal experience and his political disillusionment, runs through the collection as an easily detectable leitmotiv. De Lisle's despair with his own times turned him toward the past, and most of the verse of the *Poèmes antiques* emphasizes his attempt to replace a philosophical void by a consoling appreciation of lasting beauty. If Louis Ménard's expert guidance enabled him to arrive at a comprehensive understanding of the Greek temperament, the publication of Eugène Burnouf's *Introduction à l'histoire du bouddhisme* in 1845 and *Le Bhagâvata purâna* in 1847 initiated him into the principles of Indian and Hindu wisdom.

The presence of "Sûrya" and "Bhagavat" in the *Poèmes antiques* does considerably more than cater to the tastes of the nineteenth-century French reader who exhibited an increasing interest in Eastern philosophy at that time; the two meditations serve as testimony to de Lisle's somewhat feverish search for an acceptable interpretation of human existence. With such "Christian" poems as "Cyrille et Hypatie" and "Dies Irae" [Day of wrath] as well as with such moving exaltations of elemental forces which may be discerned in "Midi" [Noon] and in "Nox" [Night], the Indian poems reinforce dramatically the expression of overwhelming metaphysical pessimism that emerges from the collection.

Leconte de Lisle went considerably beyond the limits of Christianity and Hellenic civilization to find an acceptable substitute for the loss of a divine principle. The desire of a final absorption into nothingness, described in the ancient Sanskrit texts of the Vedas, responded most closely to the metaphysical pessimism which he personally experienced. Much has been said concerning the authenticity of the poet's scholarly reproduction of Hindu wisdom in such poems as "Bhagavat" and "Sûrya." Whatever license de Lisle may have taken in his allusions to the sacred texts need not concern the reader of his poems unduly. What matters more importantly is that the poet, through his careful attention to characteristic detail, has managed to convey in such verse as "Sûrya," for example, an evocation pregnant with mystery and colored by exoticism. The theme of the sun blends aptly with the unfamiliar symbolism of Indian mythology.

"Sûrya" recounts the legend of the god of the sun in Vedic mythology. De Lisle's poem takes on the form of a Vedic hymn of praise to the absolute power of nature. The plight of Sûrya, abandoned by his mother, the great goddess Aditi, and condemned to travel aimlessly in the heavens in a chariot drawn by seven yellow horses in search of his rightful place among the gods, appealed strongly to the poet's imagination who saw in Sûrya's predicament an analogy with man's fate. De Lisle's invocation to "the king of the world" in the closing lines of the poem betrays an awesome if not fearful expression of admiration:

> *O Sûrya! Ton corps lumineux vers l'eau noire*
> *S'incline, revêtu d'une robe de gloire;*
> *L'Abîme te salue et s'ouvre devant toi:*
> *Descends sur le profond rivage et dors, ô Roi!*
>
> *Ta demeure est au bord des océans antiques,*
> *Maître! Les grandes Eaux lavent tes pieds mystiques.*
>
> *Guerrier resplendissant, qui marches dans le ciel*
> *A travers l'étendue et le temps éternel;*
> *Toi qui verses au sein de la Terre robuste*
> *Le fleuve fécondant de ta chaleur auguste,*
> *Et sièges vers midi sur les brûlants sommets,*
> *Roi du monde, entends-nous, et protège à jamais*
> *Les hommes au sang pur, les races pacifiques*
> *Qui te chantent au bord des océans antiques!*

["Oh! Sûrya! Your luminous body inclines toward the black water and you are cloaked in a robe of glory. The abyss greets you and opens up before you: descend onto its darkest shores and sleep, my king! You reside on the banks of the ancient oceans, master! And the great waters wash your mystical feet. You are the resplendent warrior who walks in the skies across the vast expanses of eternal time, and you pour into the breast of the robust Earth the fruitful stream of your majestic warmth. At the full light of day, you sit near the burning summits. King of the world, hear and protect men of pure heart and of peaceful ways who sing to you at the shores of the ancient oceans."] The nervous alternation between the brilliant light of the sun and the darkness of the abyss conveyed through repeated contrasts of details in natural settings projects the sense of uneasiness felt by the poet who acknowledges the absolute power of nature but who suspects its indifference to the condition of man.

Central to the thematic exposition of the *Poèmes antiques* is Leconte de Lisle's rejection of Christianity as a valid religion for modern man. "Hypatie et Cyrille" contrasts Christian anxiety with classical impassibility and fulfillment. What the poet leaves unsaid in the poem concerning the nefarious influence of the Christian religion on man, he spells out in clear and almost brutal language in his *Histoire populaire du Christianisme* of 1871: "Christianity, and I mean by that every Christian communion, from Roman Catholicism to the most obscure Protestant sects, has always exercised a deplorable influence on the human intelligence. It condemns thought and dismisses reason: it has combatted against every truth systematically acquired through science. Its dogmas are unintelligible and arbitrary, and they prove indifferent to human conduct." [10]

If Christianity has any value still worth considering, maintains de Lisle, it is to be found in the art and the poetry that it has produced. "Hypatie et Cyrille" lashes out against the kind of fanaticism that would destroy beauty and science so unremittingly. Indeed, the historical figure of Hypatia is made to appear as a virtual allegory of beauty and knowledge in the poem. By so divesting all emotional appeal from his pagan martyr, de Lisle has rendered the poem too discursive, and the reader becomes painfully aware that Hypatia's speeches are treatises on the superiority of Greek polytheism over Christianity. By shifting the recitative from the more subtle indirect second person to the first person in the modified version published in the *Poèmes antiques*, de Lisle tempered significantly the emotional charge that emerged from the original poem which appeared in the July 1847 issue of the *Phalange*. Hypatia speaks in language that is singularly arid and she conveys a sense of aloofness in her philosophical exchanges with Cyril on the virtues and cultural merits of paganism.

Whatever its shortcomings, "Hypatie et Cyrille" succeeded in translating the poet's visible annoyance with religious and political institutions that continue to delude humanity by instilling belief in the existence of perfect happiness. As such, "Hypatie et Cyrille" anticipates "Le Nazaréen" of the *Poèmes barbares* and "L'Illusion suprême" of the *Poèmes tragiques*. Hypatia's final speech combines the poet's artistic appreciation of Greek paganism with a stoical outlook that will increasingly characterize his expression in the subsequent collections of poetry:

> Je ne puis oublier, en un silence lâche,
> Le soin de mon honneur et ma suprême tâche,
> Celle de confesser librement sous les cieux
> Le beau, le vrai, le bien, qu'ont révélés les Dieux.
> Depuis deux jours déjà, comme une écume vile,
> Les moines du désert abondent dans la ville,
> Pieds nus, la barbe inculte et les cheveux souillés,
> Tout maigris par le jeûne, et du soleil brûlés.
> On prétend qu'un projet sinistre et fanatique
> Amène parmi nous cette horde extatique.
> C'est bien. Je sais mourir, et suis fière du choix
> Dont m'honorent les Dieux une dernière fois.

["I cannot bring myself to forget through a cowardly silence that I have a supreme task to accomplish for the sake of my honor. I will confess proudly and openly under the heavens my belief in beauty, truth, and goodness such as these things have been revealed to me by the gods. For two days now, the monks from the desert, barefooted, with unkempt beards and with dirty hair, emanciated by fasts, and sunburned, have been swarming into the city like a vile scum. They say that a sinister and fanatical scheme brings this hysterical horde into our midst. So be it. I know how to die, and I am proud of the choice with which the gods have honored me for one last time."]

French critical reaction to the *Poèmes antiques* in December of 1852 proved to be considerably more reserved than that of some of the leading English literary observers of the time. Edmund Gosse, Arthur Symons, and Swinburne, to mention but some of the most prominent, voiced their enthusiastic endorsement of Leconte de Lisle's Parnassian verse in perceptive notices. If the French critics displayed recalcitrance in accepting the poet's particular conception of Hinduism in the collection, they lavished generous praise upon "Midi" for the plastic splendor which it evoked. They admired the poem for its impeccable form and for its excellent rhythms, and classified it as a superb example of the poet's nostalgia for his native Bourbon-Réunion Island.

Sainte-Beuve was among the few nineteenth-century critics to call attention to the fact that the closing lines of "Midi" contain a sudden yet discernible shift in attitude which changes the nature of the meditation: "In the last part, the poet translates man's supreme disillusionment in terms that are comingled with a natural setting. Then, suddenly, he leaves the sunlit landscapes of Europe and takes an unaccountable step in the direction of India." [11] Whatever else, Sainte-Beuve demonstrated keen perception in associating "Midi" with the more obvious poems belonging to the Hindu cycle. Much of the morbid attraction and charm of "Midi" stems precisely from an ironic awareness that nothingness lies beneath the elaborate formal beauty and sadness of the lines. De Lisle presents a curiously eclectic vision of existence by his mixture of elements of Darwinian transformism with Hindu attitudes.

If "Midi" emphasizes total absorption into nonbeing as the single recourse remaining for man who has been stripped of belief in a divine principle, it also acknowledges the act of an evil creator who has engendered an unquenchable taste for the absolute in man. The poem joins the other Indian poems through its conveyance of the impression that the external world remains but an illusion and that the only worthwhile wisdom that man may hope to obtain is the one which will allow him to snuff out his insatiable desire for the absolute. Renunciation of all human desire and attachment endows man with a foretaste of Nirvana and quiet repose. "Midi" illustrates admirably Leconte de Lisle's scorn for practical actuality; the poem describes the wishes of a man, spiritually fatigued by the modern world, to reach a state of calm in which he might contemplate the natural and primeval world. As such, "Midi" betrays an almost overpowering nostalgia for the past that is no more.

The opening strophes of "Midi" set the mood and the tone for the meditation that ensues. De Lisle establishes a wishful longing for rest and inactivity by his insistent allusions to the heat, light and immobility of the plain which he describes: "At noon . . . silver sheets of ardent light fall" and "the fields are not shaded." "Everything is still" is reinforced by the image of "a land asleep in its fiery blanket." Contrasting with the description of a landscape virtually annihilated by the scorching noon sun is the movement of the cornfield and of the white oxen lying on the grass. Man's absence is conspicuous throughout the poem. Through their busy practical concerns, they have deadened their intuitive response to nature. It is interesting to note the inference contained in "Midi." It is for man to imitate the example of the oxen in order to arrive at the desired state of Nirvana. The four closing strophes emphasize the poet's metaphysical pessimism:

> Non loin, quelques boeufs blancs, couchés parmi
> les herbes,

Bavent avec lenteur sur leurs fanons épais,
Et suivent de leurs yeux languissants et superbes
Le songe intérieur qu'ils n'achèvent jamais.

Homme, si, le coeur plein de joie et d'amertume,
Tu passais vers midi dans les champs radieux,
Fuis! la nature est vide et le soleil consume:
Rien n'est vivant ici, rien n'est triste ou joyeux.

Mais si, désabusé des larmes et du rire,
Altéré de l'oubli de ce monde agité,
Tu veux, ne sachant plus pardonner ou maudire,
Goûter une suprême et morne volupté,

Viens! Le soleil te parle en paroles sublimes;
Dans sa flamme implacable absorbe-toi sans fin;
Et retourne à pas lents vers les cités infimes,
Le coeur trempé sept fois dans le néant divin.

["A few white oxen lying on the grass closely are slowly
dribbling on their thick dewlaps, and their great, languid
eyes reveal the inner dream which they never finish.
Man, if you should pass by the radiant fields with your
heart filled with either joy or bitterness, run away! Nature remains indifferent and the sun consumes everything: nothing here is alive, nothing here is sad or
joyful. But if in your laughter and your tears, you are
disillusioned and if you thirst for forgetfulness of this
perturbed world, not knowing anymore how to forgive or
to curse while you wish for a taste of a last blunted
pleasure, then, come! The sun will speak to you in a
sublime language. Absorb yourself endlessly in its un-
relenting flame, and go back slowly toward the lowly
cities with your heart seven times soaked in the divine
void."]

Leconte de Lisle's statement on the relationship between man and nature emerges as more than a variant
on the theme of indifference such as it had been previously exploited by Lamartine. Vigny, Hugo, and Musset. "Midi" projects the view of a nature which acts as a
great impassive receptacle in which the Darwinian strug-

gle for survival takes place. Unlike Vigny and Hugo who unleashed emotional deprecations at nature for its apparent indifference to the needs of man, de Lisle sees in its impassibility a quality which can be transmitted to its contemplator. Nature is endowed with a hidden and appeasing virtue since it engenders in the poet a desire for ultimate absorption into the void and nothingness. If nature does not actively collaborate with the human aspiration for permanence, it serves as a liberating agent from the exasperating limits of man's individuality insomuch as it suggests an unalterable peace through absorption in its impersonalized receptacle. As such, nature restores to the individual the peace of mind which ordinary life activity has disturbed.

The closing poem of the collection, "Dies Irae," projects a vision of the end of the world which corresponds in mood and in treatment to the last poem of the *Poèmes barbares*, "Solvet seclum" ["The dissolution of the century]. The poem reinforces the thematic development of the entire volume and summarizes most successfully the precise sense of alienation experienced by the poet. "Dies Irae" equates human life with suffering that is only aggravated by the individual's identification with the unsatisfactory social organization of the ages. Leconte de Lisle states his predicament with exemplary taste and displays complete control over the powerful emotions which have doubtless inspired "Dies Irae." The allusions to his personal disappointments in life are cast within the ostensible framework of a general metaphysical meditation. There exists in the various stanzas a nearly perfect Parnassian balance between personal and generalized appreciation of the human condition.[12]

"Dies Irae" projects a powerful and conclusive rejection of contemporary values and reasserts in memorable terms the nature of de Lisle's metaphysical pessimism:

Mais, si rien ne répond dans l'immense étendue,
Que le stérile écho de l'éternel Désir,

Adieu, déserts, où l'âme ouvre une aile éperdue!
Adieu, songe sublime, impossible à saisir!

Et toi, divine Mort, où tout rentre et s'efface,
Accueille tes enfants dans ton sein étoilé;
Affranchis-nous du temps, du nombre et de l'espace,
Et rend-nous le repos que la vie a troublé!

["But if nothing responds in the vast expanse of time
and space except the sterile echo of man's futile desire
for eternity, then, goodbye, deserts in which the soul
first spread its bewildered wing. Adieu, sublime dream
which has been impossible to contain. And you, divine
Death into which everything enters and becomes ob-
literated, receive your children in your starry breast.
Deliver us from the tyranny of time, finite number and
of space, and give back to us the deep repose which life
has taken from us."]

The *Poèmes barbares*, which enjoyed three separate
editions from 1862 to 1878,[13] pursued Leconte de Lisle's
scholarly examination of the ancient beliefs and traditions which contributed in establishing the various
Western and Eastern civilizations. The seventy-seven
poems which comprise the definitive edition of 1878
stray from the idealized Greek and Hindu world of the
Poèmes antiques, and concentrate upon other civilizations considered semibarbaric or even barbaric by the
poet. De Lisle has recourse to the various myths and
legends associated with the Scandinavian countries,
Spain, biblical history, and the Christian Middle Ages.
Much of the narrative verse that contrasts the superiority of ancient barbarism over the epochs immediately
preceding our own frequently possesses an epic quality.
The poems concerned with Scandinavian warriors, revolutionaries in biblical times, and wild animals that in-
habit forests and jungles are endowed with a sense of
beauty and grandeur that is noticeably absent from the
poems dealing with the Middle Ages, for example.
De Lisle's prejudice against Christianity causes him
to abandon legend for history as he touches upon the

Middle Ages and comes closer to modern times. Anatole France has criticized the poet for viewing the Christian era with an obvious single-mindedness: "M. Leconte de Lisle sees only famines, ignorance, leprosy, and burning stakes. . . ." [14] More than anything else, the *Poèmes barbares* underscore the fanaticism and the bloodshed which have punctuated the history of humanity since Greek and Hindu antiquity. The poems of the collection verify de Lisle's earlier pessimism and charge his invocations to death with a chillingly dramatic intensity.

That Leconte de Lisle may have somewhat literally transcribed a number of Xavier Marmier's *Chants populaires du nord* [Popular Nordic legends] of 1842 in the *Poèmes barbares* should not distract us from the serious task of evaluating his verse for its own poetic effectiveness. [15] The unalterable fact remains that despite certain borrowings from Marmier and Léouzon-le-Duc's *Légendes finnoises*, de Lisle's poetic renderings constitute a decidedly noticeable improvement over the often grossly comic and mawkish accounts of the two French folklorists. The poet's obvious fascination with Scandinavian myths stemmed logically from the distinctly anti-Christian flavor and from the pessimistic predictions embodied in the legends of the three nornes, Urd, Verdandi, and Skulda.

According to ancient Scandinavian lore, the world was destined to be destroyed and to be reborn from the surging waters of the ocean. De Lisle understandably manifested sustained interest in the legend of Skulda, the third norne whose predictions of the future described the world's imminent demise and the engulfment of all of creation into nothingness. "L'Illusion suprême" and "La Vision de Snorr," to mention but the two most striking poems in the collection, are somber recastings of the Scandinavian myths which had been popularized by Marmier. However derivative the *Poèmes barbares* may strike us as reworkings of the folklorist's tales, many of the individual poems emerge as veritable poetic creations far superior to their source, the *Chants populaires du nord.*

Of all Leconte de Lisle's verse, no other poem enjoyed such wide popular acceptance as "Le Coeur d'Hialmar," which appeared in the January, 1864, issue of the *Revue contemporaine* before being inserted into the 1872 edition of the *Poèmes barbares.* For all of its formal perfection, "Le Coeur d'Hialmar" [The heart of Hialmar] emerges as a stunning evocation of the primitive grandeur and the stoical heroism which the poet has chosen to associate with the warriors of ancient Scandinavia. The sonorously metallic quality of the language appears admirably suited to the harshness and fierceness of the tableau which depicts the brave warrior, Hialmar, dying in the midst of his own deceased soldiers. The stark juxtaposition of scenes which alternatively evoke life and death endows the poem with a certain tragic and epic sense. De Lisle achieves an effective visual impression from the beginning which he manages to sustain throughout "Le Coeur d'Hialmar." The opening lines, for example, describe an eerie landscape setting by the lugubrious light of the moon: the white of the snow contrasts hauntingly with the red blood of the dead soldiers and the black of the unremitting vultures that plane overhead in the dark indifference of the night.

Against this chilling backdrop, the dying Hialmar enters into a monologue before his dead soldiers, and then addresses a vulture nearby because he feels he has a last compelling mission to accomplish before his death. So that his fiancée may know of his love for her and so that she may remember him always with pride, he commands the crow to tear out his heart and take it to the daughter of Ylmer in Upsala. De Lisle has succeeded handsomely in approximating the stilted speech of the fearless warrior, accustomed more to directness in expression and ignorant of the subtle art of periphrasis. Yet the barbaric proposition which he makes translates an unmistakably innate nobility and purity of heart, given the fact that his dying thoughts envelop the woman he loves in touching tenderness. Hialmar prepares himself to face death stoically, and his parting words betray a great pride:

Viens par ici, Corbeau, mon brave mangeur d'hommes,
Ouvre-moi la poitrine avec ton bec de fer.
Tu nous retrouveras demain tels que nous sommes.
Porte mon coeur tout chaud à la fille d'Ylmer.

.   .   .   .

Va, sombre messager, dis-lui bien que je l'aime,
Et que voici mon coeur. Elle reconnaîtra
Qu'il est rouge et solide et non tremblant et blême;
Et la fille d'Ylmer, Corbeau, te sourira!

Moi, je meurs. Mon esprit coule par vingt blessures.
J'ai fait mon temps. Buvez, ô loups, mon sang vermeil.
Jeune, brave, riant, libre et sans flétrissures,
Je vais m'asseoir parmi les Dieux, dans le soleil!

["Come here, Crow, my brave scavanger of the flesh of men, open my breast with your iron beak. You will find us still here tomorrow just as we are now. Carry my warm heart to Ylmer's daughter. . . . Go, messenger of death, and be sure to tell her that I love her very much, and that I am sending her my heart. And when she recognizes that it is crimson red and hardy, and not trembling and pale, Ylmer's daughter will smile in gratitude at you. As for myself, I shall die. My spirit flows in the twenty wounds that I have received. I have lived my life. Wolves, drink my dark red blood. Young, brave, laughing, free and unblemished, I go to take my place among the gods in the sun!"]

"Le Coeur d'Hialmar" through its alternation of darkness with light (the first and last words of the poem are *night* and *sun*), renders a highly pictorial account of the theme which is developed. The richness of detail so prominently evident endows the tableau with a vivid sculptural motif. The simplicity of the rhythm, which pursues a steady and deliberate pace throughout the poem, blends perfectly with the austere manner in which de Lisle relates the heroism of his barbaric warrior. But it is principally the forcefulness of the poet's imagination that invests "Le Coeur d'Hialmar" with its most convincing intrinsic unity. From beginning to end, Hialmar remains the awesome creation of the poet's imaginative powers: these narrated verses cast a spell upon the reader which projects him momentarily into the imaginative universe of Leconte de Lisle. "Le Coeur d'Hialmar" betrays the poet's single-minded determination to evoke a primeval and barbaric epoch which has never really existed in historical fact.

For all of the realistic traits that adorn the descriptive tableaus, "Le Coeur d'Hialmar" is too heavily impregnated with a high-blown idealism for it to emerge as a believable account of the ancient Scandinavian warrior. For all of its realistic technique, the poem conveys an unreal conception of the world. The poem owes its overall effectiveness to a poetic imagination tempered or modified by at least an outward reference to the periphery of reality and history.

First published in the November 1847 issue of the *Phalange*, "La Fontaine aux lianes" [The fountain and the liana creepers] is the earliest known poem which nostalgically recalls Leconte de Lisle's native island of La Réunion. In theme and treatment, "La Fontaine aux lianes" joins "Sûrya" of the *Poèmes antiques*, yet its inclusion in the collection on the barbaric races may be justified by its extolment of a luxuriant primitive nature. The poem virtually teems with the poet's ostensibly implacable acceptance of the seemingly unalterable laws of nature. The emotion that emanates from these verses is couched in de Lisle's complicated notion of nature's relationship to man. If nature emerges as something essentially indifferent and benevolent, it is primarily because death engenders in man a sense of anguish and generates in him a strangely serene resignation. The nature of the poem's stated nostalgia for the past recalls the highly charged reminiscences of Nerval's

"Fantaisie" in the *Odelettes* and of Baudelaire's "La Vie antérieure" [The prior existence] in the *Fleurs du Mal*. The recollection of the resplendent island that Leconte de Lisle knew during his youth awakens in him an obsessive desire to return to the past which his creative imagination has reframed in the light of later experiences and disappointments.

"La Fontaine aux lianes" symbolically revives a more metaphysical longing within the poet: it translates with quivering implicitness the yearning to return to the prenatal state in which the excruciating awareness of being is eradicated by an untroubled void.

Au fond des bois baignés d'une vapeur céleste,
Il était une eau vive où rien ne remuait;
Quelques joncs verts, gardiens de la fontaine agreste,
S'y penchaient au hasard en un groupe muet.

Les larges nénuphars, les lianes errantes,
Blancs archipels, flottaient enlacés sur les eaux,
Et dans leurs profondeurs vives et transparantes
Brillait un autre ciel où nageaient les oiseaux.

O fraîcheur des forêts, sérénité première,
O vents qui caressiez les feuillages chanteurs,
Fontaine aux flots heureux où jouait la lumière,
Eden épanoui sur les vertes hauteurs.

Salut, ô douce paix, et vous, pures haleines,
Et vous qui descendiez du ciel et des rameaux,
Repos du coeur, oubli de la joie et des peines!
Salut! ô sanctuaire interdit à nos maux!

["In the depths of the woods which were bathed in a celestial morning dew, there used to be a spring tide in which nothing stirred; only a few sweet rushes, keepers of the rustic fountain, would lean over the water in silent testimony. The large water lilies and the creeping liana, like white archipelagos, would float in interlacing fashion on the waters whose deep transparency reflected the brilliance of another sky in which birds

swam. Oh! coolness of the forests, reminiscence of the
ultimate serenity; oh! winds which would caress the
singing leaves, fountain whose waves played with the
sunlight, Eden extended to the green eminences, I greet
you. And you, gentle peace; and you, pure breaths drawn
from the heavens and from the reeds. Solace for my
heart, forgetfulness of human joy and tribulations! I
greet you, sanctuary from which our sufferings are excluded!"]

For many critics, Leconte de Lisle's surest claim to
posterity rested upon a number of verses in the *Poèmes
barbares* and in the *Poèmes tragiques* which evoked
lush nature settings and exotic jungles inhabited by wild
animals. The so-called animal poems are deft portraits
of primitivism, the obvious product of the poet's astute
observations of the menagerie contained in the Parisian
zoological gardens. De Lisle's animal poems are strik-
ingly conceived and brilliantly realized: only the most
characteristic traits and details are utilized to reveal an
aesthetic and symbolic attitude. Baudelaire hailed the
poet's exotic evocations and animal portraits as his most
distinguished achievement: ". . . the poet has described beauty such as it has manifested itself to him:
the dignified, crushing forces of nature, the majesty of
animals in motion and at rest . . . finally, the serenity
of the desert or the magnificence of the ocean. In such
instances, Leconte de Lisle proves to be a master and a
great master." [16]

Such poems as "Les Eléphants," "Le Sommeil du
condor" [The condor's sleep], "La Panthère noire,"
[The black panther], "Le Rêve du jaguar" [The Jaguar's dream], "L'Abatros," and "L'Incantation du
loup" [The wolf's incantation], to mention but the
best known of the series, recall the archaic world of
primitivism with admiration and eloquence. In "Les
Eléphants," for instance, de Lisle expresses what he
feels in relationship to the elemental instincts of the
animals in their sacred pilgrimage to the land of their
origin. Through the skilful deployment of the poet's

imagination, the reader catches a startling glimpse of the elephant's nostalgia for a primitive existence. Unlike the anthropomorphic wolf of Vigny and the albatross of Baudelaire, de Lisle's elephants and animals are portrayed in their primitivism. Although the poem's theme is made to reflect the poet's metaphysical nostalgia for the state of nonbeing, the portrait of the animals in their sluggish yet determined march through the desert captures a certain animalistic intuition which adds to the poetic effectiveness of the verses. Vigny's wolf and Baudelaire's albatross possess few if any genuine animalistic qualities; the wolf incarnates a human symbol for stoicism, and the albatross is no longer a bird but a poet. De Lisle's animal poems, by contrast, are more richly implicit, thematically speaking, and consequently they are far more poetic than "La Mort du Loup" [The death of the wolf] and "L'Albatros" of Vigny and Baudelaire respectively.

In "Le Sommeil du condor," we experience both the visual and auditory ascension of the great vulture as it flees higher and higher from the encompassing shadows of the night. The solitary condor's precarious position between the black abyss of the Cordilleras ranges in the Andes and the dizzying height of the summits upon which he is perched provides a fitting setting for the dramatic conflict that ensues between the light of day and the darkness of the night. The reader visualizes through the haughty and impassive gaze of the lonely condor the terrifying spectacle of summit after summit being engulfed into a pervading black abyss. The surge of energy with which the mighty bird escapes the all-encompassing darkness toward the beckoning light of the Southern Cross is conveyed with remarkable dexterity:

> Du continent muet elle s'est emparée:
> Des sables aux coteaux, des gorges aux versants,
> De cime en cime, elle enfle, en tourbillons croissants,
> Le lourd débordement de sa haute marée.

Lui, comme un spectre, seul, au front du pic altier,
Baigné d'une lueur qui saigne sur la neige,
Il attend cette mer sinistre qui l'assiège:
Elle arrive, déferle, et le couvre en entier.

Dans l'abîme, sans fond la Croix australe allume
Sur les côtes du ciel son phare constellé.
Il râle de plaisir, il agite sa plume,
Il érige son cou musculeux et pelé,

Il s'enlève en fouettant l'âpre neige des Andes,
Dans un cri rauque il monte où n'atteint pas le vent,
Et, loin du globe noir, loin de l'astre vivant,
Il dort dans l'air glacé, les ailes toutes grandes.

["And the darkness takes hold of the silent continent: from the sands to the hillsides, from the gorges to the mountain sides. From summit to summit, it swells in increasing swirls the heavy overflowing of its high tide. He, like an apparition, alone at the top of the highest peak, basking in the last rays of light which bleed upon the snow, awaits this sinister sea of darkness which will beseige him: it arrives, unfurls itself, and covers him completely. In the endless abyss of obscurity, the Southern Cross illumines the edges of the sky with its flashing constellation. He gasps with pleasure, stirs up his plumage, raises his peeled, muscular neck, and rises in the air while lashing away at the bitterly cold snow of the Andes. With a raucous cry, he ascends to heights which the winds cannot attain, and far from the darkened globe and from the living star, he sleeps in the icy air with his magnificent wings outstretched."]

De Lisle's use of the long alexandrine line with the regular alternation of masculine and feminine rhymes produces a lingering auditory effect which corresponds superbly with the visual tableau of vast expanses of space and the dignified solitude of the impassive condor. The verse possesses the same kind of nervous concision and energy that is conveyed in William Blake's "The Tyger" from the *Songs of Experience*. The condor's preparation for the flight and his majestic ascension into the heights of the awesome mountain peaks is splendidly evoked through a few characteristic traits which enable the reader's imagination to soar with the bird's poetic escape from the encompassing darkness. As with the other animal poems, Leconte de Lisle displays his expertise in the effective use of periphrasis in "Le Sommeil du condor." His albatross, wolf, jaguar, and condor all succeed in evoking the grandiose, archaic world of primitivism as they recall with memorable indirection the attitude of passivity and detachment of the French Parnassian poet. De Lisle makes his point all the more forcefully since he bequeaths his animals an urgent primeval dignity.

"La Vérandah," published initially in the 1866 issue of the *Parnasse contemporain* and subsequently inserted in the 1872 edition of the *Poèmes barbares*, displays the unusual technical finesse with which Leconte de Lisle was frequently capable of obtaining striking thematic effects in his poetry. "La Vérandah" illustrates his adroit handling of the envelope motif in the rarely used difficult seven-line strophe.[17] The skilful manipulation of rhyme, rhythm, and meter conjures up a ghostly atmosphere of what the poet means by an archaic and prehistoric stillness. Whatever his motivation, his poem translates in compellingly urgent language the sense of an absolute silence which is virtually hypnotic and narcotic:

Sous les treillis d'argent de la vérandah close,
Dans l'air tiède embaumé de l'odeur des jasmins,
Où la splendeur du jour darde une flèche rose,
La Persane royale, immobile, repose,
Derrière son col brun croisant ses belles mains,
Dans l'air tiède, embaumé de l'odeur des jasmins,
Sous les treillis d'argent de la vérandah close.

. . . .

Et l'eau vive s'endort dans les porphyres roux,

Les rosiers de l'Iran ont cessé leurs murmures,
Et les ramiers rêveurs leurs roucoulements doux.
Tout se tait. L'oiseau grêle et le frelon jaloux
Ne se querellent plus autour des figues mûres.
Les rosiers de l'Iran ont cessé leurs murmures,
Et l'eau vive s'endort dans les porphyres roux.

["Under the silvery trellis of the enclosed verandah, the
tepid air is embalmed with the smell of the jasmines
and the day's splendor shoots forth a pink arrow. The
royal Persian lady is perfectly still and resting behind
her exposed brown neck and her folded arms in the tepid
air which is embalmed with the smell of the jasmines
under the silvery trellis of the enclosed verandah. . . .
And the spring tide drops off to sleep in the midst of the
reddish-brown porphyry; the rose trees of Iran have
ceased their murmurings and the dreamy ringdoves
their soft cooings. Everything becomes silent. The
slender bird and the jealous hornet no longer quarrel
around the ripe fig trees. The rose trees of Iran have
ceased their murmurings and the spring tide drops off
to sleep in the midst of the reddish-brown porphyry."]

Of Leconte de Lisle's entire poetic production, the
poems concerned with the Christian Middle Ages come
closest to unveiling the polemical spirit that inspired
them. If from the points of view of tone and thematic
treatment de Lisle's "Le Nazaréen" [The Nazarene]
may be approximated and compared with Nerval's
five sonnets in the Chimères, called, "Le Christ aux
Oliviers," such poems as "Le Corbeau" [The crow]
in the Poèmes barbares predict the emotionally vitu-
perative "Les Siècles maudits" [The damned centuries]
of the Poèmes tragiques. In "Le Corbeau," Mephistoph-
eles recounts Christ's agony and death; the crow under-
takes the double function of philosopher and artist.
The rapacious vulture is about to pick at the cadaver of
Christ when an angel prevents him in time from dis-
figuring the beautiful head of the crucified Messiah.
More poetically effective is the minor epic realized in

the dramatic account of Qaïn who stands as the tragic symbol of the revolutionary spirit during biblical times.

The theme of revolt against the arbitrary construction of an essential universe devised by the religious values found in basic Judeo-Christian tradition found its way into the prose and poetry of such noted Romanticists as Goethe, Byron, Hugo, Baudelaire, and Nerval. The Romantic appetite for personalization of familiar legends led writers logically to an exploitation of the myth of Prometheus in their attempts to reinterpret the human predicament more meaningfully. The story of Cain, the first revolutionary spirit of biblical literature, provided an important corollary to the meaning they had assigned to the legend of Prometheus. Yet the myth of Cain, unlike that of Prometheus, was complicated by reference to the Christian God of the nineteenth century, and such Romanticists as Hugo, Baudelaire, and Nerval responded with detectable reservation in affirming Cain's revolt against the Creator and his awful murder of Abel.

If Leconte de Lisle's *Qaïn* differed significantly from the various Romantic evocations of the biblical figure, it was principally through the exacting care and technique with which he managed to achieve a subdued lyrical quality in his epic poem. Thematically, the difference between his Cain and Vigny's Moses or Goethe's Prometheus is negligible. A comparison between Byron's dramatic poem, *Cain: A Mystery*, first published in 1821, and de Lisle's *Qaïn* gives sharper perspective to the aesthetic distance which separated the Romantic from the Parnassian approach to the legend. Byron's poem, like the interpretations of most of his Romantic congeners, is rooted basically in the acceptance of inherited forms of Christian theology. Byron's dramatic poem unfolds a tension existing not so much between two protagonists as between the alternatives for ideas and beliefs which they purport to represent. *Cain: A Mystery* establishes the required tension dramatically in the first canto through the philosophical dialogue between Adam and Cain: "Dost thou not *live?*" asks the first man; "Must I not *die?*" retorts the rebellious son. There remains in Byron's Cain something of the wrathful brother encountered in Genesis who nurtures metaphysical reservation concerning the finite nature of man's physical existence. De Lisle's poem translates a more ambitious epic intention since it reaches out to portray both the beginnings of a race and its ultimate annihilation by the great Deluge.

Qaïn resorts ingeniously to the device of incorporating the entire biblical story into the dreams of the seer, Thogorma, who relates the events of the hundreds of years that have passed since the time of the Garden of Eden to the Flood. Thogorma serves in the double capacity of prophet and narrator since he tells of that which took place before and after his own time. The poet's design becomes readily obvious from the opening lines: de Lisle emphasizes the dismay, the suffering and the despair experienced by a people whose faith in Iahvèh remains basically unsubstantiated.

One of the most effective sequences in this lengthy epic poem is the narrative segment which describes the original innocence of the earth and the primitive, uncorrupted love of life in the Garden of Eden. In a vision of the time of the earth's creation, Thogorma relates that he sees primitive men, pagans and consequently freed of the tyranny of God, who have succeeded in dominating nature, containing animals for their use, and who live in harmonious community. In still another vision, Thogorma witnesses Qaïn as he rises from the grave on the earth that has imprisoned him. The wailing forests and the terrified mountains which surround him infuse the passage with an undeniable dramatic intensity. In a parodistic inversion of Christ's resurrection, Qaïn rises from the dead to decry God's injustice to man. Qaïn replies to the sentinel, Khéroub, who reproaches him for his defiance in language that defines the nature of his revolt in unmistakable terms:

Je resterai debout! Et du soir à l'aurore,
Et de l'aube à la nuit, jamais je ne tairai
L'infatigable cri d'un coeur désespéré!
La soif de la justice, ô Khéroub, me dévore.
Ecrase-moi, sinon, jamais je ne ploîrai!

Ténèbres, répondez! Qu'Iahvèh me réponde!
Je souffre, qu'ai-je fait?—Le Khéroub dit:—Qaïn!
Iahvèh l'a voulu. Tais-toi. Fais ton chemin
Terrible.—Sombre Esprit, le mal est dans le monde.
Oh! pourquoi suis-je né!—Tu le sauras demain.—

Je l'ai su. Comme l'ours aveuglé qui trébuche
Dans la fosse où la mort l'a longtemps attendu,
Flagellé de fureur, ivre, sourd, éperdu,
J'ai heurté d'Iahvèh l'inévitable embûche;
Il m'a précipité dans le crime tendu.

O jeune homme, tes yeux, tels qu'un ciel sans nuage,
Etaient calmes et doux, ton coeur était léger
Comme l'agneau qui sort de l'enclos du berger;
Et Celui qui te fit docile à l'esclavage
Par ma main violente a voulu t'égorger.

["I shall remain standing! And from night until dawn
and from dawn until night, I will never cease to eject
tirelessly the anguished cry of a soul in despair! Thirst
for justice, Khéroub, consumes me. Crush me, for I
shall never submit! Darkness, answer me. Let Iahvèh
answer me! I suffer. What have I done?—The sentinel
says: Qaïn! Iahvèh has willed it so. Be quiet, and go
your terrible way.—Dark Spirit of the night, evil resides
in the world. Oh! why was I born!—You will know
why tomorrow.—I did learn the reason. Like the blinded
bear who staggers into the trench where death has been
awaiting him for a longtime, beaten into a crazed anger,
drunk, deaf, bewildered, I stumbled into Iahvèh's inevitable ambush; he pushed me to commit the crime for
which I had been created to commit. Oh! young man,
your eyes, like that of the clear blue sky, were soft and
calm, your heart was light like that of the lamb which

leaves the shepherd's enclosure, and He who made you docile to enslavement has willed that you should be strangled by my violent hand."]

In Qaïn, Leconte de Lisle found a fitting spokesman to propound the views and the attitudes which reside at the basis of all of his poetry. In a speech to posterity, Qaïn denounces men who acquiesce to live in cowardly and servile bondage to an imperfect Creator. He promises that his revolutionary spirit will live in dedicated activity to throw off the yoke of subjugation. Qaïn formulates the philosophical attitude contained in embryonic fashion in still another poem from the collection on the barbaric races, "La Tristesse du diable" [The sadness of the devil]. De Lisle redefines the Satan so familiar to the Romanticists in one verse as "the first dreamer and the oldest victim." Like Nerval's Cain in the "Legend of Adoniram" in the *Voyage en orient* of 1851, de Lisle's Qaïn escapes the great Flood. The seer Thogorma in his dream recalls the rebel escaping the murderous waters. Like Nerval's Cain, Qaïn emerges as the clear and tragic symbol of the anarchistic spirit which survives in the modern age. Qaïn of Leconte de Lisle descends from a Romantic tradition of rebels and revolutionaries conceived in classical and biblical mythology.

The real force of Leconte de Lisle's Qaïn lies in its poetic and dramatic articulation of the human condition bequeathed man from the time of the first biblical revolt in Genesis. For the most part, the poet eschews the recounting of biblical events for their own sake. Whatever discernible sequential order is maintained serves as a kind of dramatic backdrop for the epic: de Lisle is obviously more concerned with investing Qaïn with an intense lyrical dimension. His well-known propensity for scholarly documentation and method asserts itself by the retention of original spellings for the names of such biblical figures as Iahvèh, Khaldée, Héva, Qaïn. More frequently than not, such technical precision lends a heightened austerity to the poem, and only in rare instances does it actually detract from the internal poetic continuity of the epic. The lyricism which is achieved differs substantively from that obtained in Byron's *Cain: A Mystery* insomuch as it tends to transcend the immediacy of the scriptural account and extend into a more generalized lamentation on the human predicament. The effectiveness or ineffectiveness of lyrical expression is largely dependent upon the type of rhetorical and technical expedients to which the poet has recourse in order to convince his reader of the reality of the sentiments that he wishes to convey. By and large, *Qaïn* succeeds in welding a sense of pathos to the portrait of the defiant biblical figure that permits the reader to appreciate the sincerity of Cain as well as that of the poet who transmits the impression that he himself shares a measure of the rebel's plight. In *Qaïn*, Leconte de Lisle has written the apology for modern revolt. Anatole France went so far as to see in *Qaïn* a thinly disguised portrait of the Parnassian poet himself.[18]

"Solvet seclum" [The world dissolved] like "Dies Irae" in the *Poèmes antiques* derives its primary inspiration from the words of the funeral hymn composed in the thirteenth century and subsequently inserted in the mass for the dead. "Solvet seclum" projects the poet's intuitive vision of the end of the world in despairing, nihilistic terms. The raucous and almost rasping sound suggested in the rhythm of de Lisle's recitation of the desolation that he envisions endows the verse with an expressive intensity even though it may lack any convincing identification with the poet. "Solvet seclum" depends upon external effects to convey in general terms the notion of a world engulfed into nothingness.

The poem closes appropriately if not altogether effectively the collection which described the degenerative descent of man from the idealized Antiquity of the Greeks and the Indians to modernism.

> Et ce ne sera point, sous les cieux magnifiques,
> Le bonheur reconquis des paradis antiques
> Ni l'entretien d'Adam et d'Eve sur les fleurs,

Ni le divin sommeil après tant de douleurs;
Ce sera quand le Globe et tout ce qui l'habite,
Bloc stérile arraché de son immense orbite,
Stupide, aveugle, plein d'un dernier hurlement,
Plus lourd, plus éperdu de moment en moment,
Contre quelque univers immobile en sa force
Défoncera sa vieille et misérable écorce,
Et, laissant ruisseler, par mille trous béants,
Sa flamme intérieure avec ses océans,
Ira fertiliser de ses restes immondes
Les sillons de l'espace où fermentent les mondes.

["And there shall not be under magnificent skies any refound happiness of ancient paradises, or any conversations between Adam and Eve on flowers, or any divine sleep after so much suffering. The end of the world will take place when the globe and all of that which inhabits it shall be pulled out of its immense orbit like a sterile block. Stupid, blind, and with one last howl, it will become heavier and more bewildered with each moment, and will catapult itself against some motionless universe in its blind force which shall shatter its old and wretched shell while it allows to trickle from a thousand gaping holes the inner flame of its oceans. Its unspeakable remains shall fertilize the furrows of space where worlds ferment."]

The *Poèmes tragiques*, which appeared in 1884, contained some thirty-seven verse narratives which pursued in harsher terms still the ideas and attitudes conveyed already in the *Poèmes antiques* and in the *Poèmes barbares*. Aside from a few effective animal poems like "L'Albatros" and "La Chasse de l'aigle" [The eagle's hunt], de Lisle's third collection of poems aimed especially at denouncing the fanaticism engendered by the various religions of the world. Both "L' Holocaust" and "Les Siècles maudits" [The accursed centuries] express bitter disdain and downright hatred for the Middle Ages that nurtured the growth of Christianity. The last poem, in particular, displays the poet's contempt for the religion whose effects he analyzed in his own nineteenth-century context.

A few lines suffice to illustrate the loss of control, emotionally and historically, of de Lisle in his appraisal of the Middle Ages. His condemnation of Christianity is as absolute and as categorical as the religious dogmas which he denounces.

> L'écume de la rage aux dents, la torche en main,
> Soufflant dans toute chair, dans toute âme vivante,
> L'angoisse d'être au monde autant que l'épouvante
> De la mort, voue au feu stupide de l'Enfer
> L'holocauste fumant sur son autel de fer!
> Dans chacune de vos exécrables minutes,
> O siècles d'égorgeurs, de lâches et de brutes,
> Honte de ce vieux globe et de l'humanité,
> Maudits, soyez maudits, et pour l'éternité!

["Frothing with enraged teeth and with torch in hand, branding upon all flesh and upon every living soul the anguish of being in the world and the terror of death, (the Christian Middle Ages) consecrate to the stupid fire of Hell a smoldering holocaust on the iron-clad altar! For each one of your despicable moments, oh! centuries of murderers, cowards, and brutes, the shame of this old globe and of humanity, may you be damned, and damned for all eternity!"]

If the heart of man remains the source of all illusion, de Lisle finds sources of earthly wisdom in Eastern thought and attitudes. "La Maya" predicts the summation of the poet's philosophical disposition which will receive its fullest expression in the striking poem, "La Paix des dieux" [The peace of the gods], first published in the *Revue des Deux Mondes* and subsequently included in the posthumous collection published under the editorship of José-Maria de Heredia in 1895.

If "La Paix des dieux" illustrates to what degree Leconte de Lisle was capable of magnifying his visionary and historical imagination toward the end of his life, the villanella "Dans l'air léger" [In the cool air] demonstrates that his concern with form, for the most part, dominated the themes and attitudes expounded in his poetry. The sadness that emanates from "Dans l'air léger" belies the sophisticated formal organization of the villanella. The villanella, a poetic form used during the Renaissance by such poets as Passerat, contains a variable number of tercets which are built on two rhymes. The original significance ascribed the term was that of a slow dance. De Lisle utilizes this classical form to frame a serious subject in "Dans l'air léger."

> Dans l'air léger, dans l'azur rose,
> Un grêle fil d'or rampe et luit
> Sur les mornes que l'aube arrose.
>
> Fleur ailée, au matin éclose,
> L'oiseau s'éveille, vole et fuit,
> Dans l'air léger, dans l'azur rose.
>
> L'abeille boit ton âme, ô rose!
> L'épais tamarinier bruit
> Sur les mornes que l'aube arrose.
>
> . . . .
> Et la mer, où le ciel repose,
> Fait monter son vaste et doux bruit
> Sur les mornes que l'aube arrose.
>
> Mais les yeux divins que j'aimais
> Se sont fermés, et pour jamais,
> Dans l'air léger, dans l'azur rose.

["In the cool air, in the pink blue sky, a slender golden thread creeps up and glitters on the bluffs which the dawn sprays. Winged flower which blossoms in the morning, the bird awakens and flies away in the cool air, in the pink blue sky. Oh! rose, the bee is drinking up your soul! The tamarind-tree makes noises on the bluffs which the dawn sprays. . . . And the sea, where the sky rests, lets its vast and gentle sound ascend to the bluffs which the dawn sprays. But the divine eyes which I loved have closed themselves for always in the cool air, in the pink blue sky."]

The poet's direct emotion is delicately contained within the formal elegance of the villanella. The frailty of the thin golden thread and the allusion to the evaporation of the rose's perfume reinforce with effective indirection the final statement on death in the closing tercet.

From the time Leconte de Lisle initially read Louis Ménard's treatise, *Du Polythéisme hellénique* [Concerning Hellenic polytheism], in 1863 to the formulation of his final philosophical outlook in 1888 when "La Paix des dieux" first appeared, he had, himself, surveyed rather comprehensively the religions and the civilizations of ancient and modern man. This long rambling poem constitutes the poet's philosophic legacy to posterity: like all men anxious to reach out and to find some palatable solution to the human enigma, de Lisle admits that his appraisal of the world's religions was steeped both in a desire for personal psychological liberation from superstition and fanaticism as well in the hope of finding faith in an eternal principle.

"La Paix des dieux" possesses a rhythm that simulates or suggests the almost rasp quality of the human voice declaiming the history of a final disillusionment. The gods of man remain the created illusions of his own desperate imagination.

> Rien ne te rendra plus la foi ni le blasphème,
> La haine, ni l'amour, et tu sais désormais,
> Eveillé brusquement en face de toi-même,
> Que ces spectres d'un jour c'est toi qui les créais.
>
> Mais va! Console-toi de ton oeuvre insensée.
> Bientôt ce vieux mirage aura fui de tes yeux,
> Et tout disparaîtra, le monde et la pensée,
> Dans l'immuable paix où sont rentrés les Dieux.

["Nothing will ever restore your faith: not blasphemy, not hatred, nor love; and you know that henceforth, having suddenly taken stock of yourself, that these spectres of the past were created by you. But, go! Don't despair of your senseless invention. This old mirage will soon flee from your eyes, and all shall disappear, the world and your thoughts, in the unalterable peace into which the gods have returned."]

Consideration of Leconte de Lisle's verse from the *Poèmes antiques* to the *Derniers poèmes* reveals the keen sense of responsibility with which he attempted to achieve the aesthetic objectives of the Parnassian school. His lyric is nourished by a conscious, self-imposed discipline that seeks to blend harmoniously ideas and sentiments with balanced metrical versification. Unlike the Symbolists which followed him, de Lisle leaves little room for ambiguity in his poems since he proceeds by statement rather than by symbol to convey the attitude or the impression which he seeks to communicate. Beneath the meticulousness or rigidity of form in his verse, there frequently escapes a sense of nostalgia or revolt which infuses his best poems with the indelible stamp of genuine lyricism. Historically, de Lisle's poetry may be said to intervene between the Romantic excesses of the 1830s and 1840s and the Symbolist subjectivism of the 1880s and 1890s. For all of its erudition and scholarly concern, the best poems of Leconte de Lisle still impose themselves today by their timeliness.

5

José-Maria de Heredia and the Poetics of Historicity

When José-Maria de Heredia published the one hundred and eighteen sonnets which comprise his single volume of verse, *Les Trophées* [The trophies] in 1893, critical reaction proved nearly unanimous in acclaiming him the most ideal and proficient practitioner of Art for Art's Sake in France. More than any other writer, Heredia had realized the aesthetic goals of Parnassianism concerning pure art and objectivity in his collection of sonnets, most of which had appeared previously in such journals as the *Revue française*, the *Revue de Paris*, and in the three editions of the *Parnasse contemporain*.

Unlike Hugo's ambitious enterprise with the epic, *La Légende des siècles*, Heredia's *Trophées* deliberately eschewed the visionary and apocalyptic interpretations on human progress in favor of more artistic and objective depiction of scenes from past civilizations worthy of modern emulation and veneration. What Heredia sought to record in his epic poems was the urgent sense of heroic human activity which has characterized the great epochs of history. As its title suggests, *Les Trophées* celebrate man's noblest and most admirable endeavor; the individual sonnets make no attempt to illustrate points of view or to prove given theses. To avoid emotional involvement, Heredia subscribed to the same Parnassian preference for the ancient and the remote as Gautier and Leconte de Lisle; *Les Trophées* come no closer than the Renaissance to the modern era.

The training Heredia had acquired in archaeology and paleography at the Ecole des Chartes taught him to substantiate his enthusiasm for the past by scientific fact rather than by personal response to a given historical event. *Les Trophées* bear the indelible stamp of the conscious workmanship of both the artist and the architect: each sonnet succeeds in evoking with apt vividness and striking accuracy the ethos of various civilizations of the past.

Considered as the most impersonal and contained of the French Parnassian poets, Heredia scrupulously refrained from intervening emotionally in his poetic mosaics of the past. He explained in particularly telling terms his own conception of the lyric in the 1894 address of acceptance to the French Academy: "True poetry rests in nature and in an unchanging humanity, and not in the fickle heart of man, however great he may be. The more impersonal a poet becomes, the more he reaches out to express humanity." His view of the function of lyricism led him naturally to select the restricted form of the sonnet for his epic evocations of the past. Concentration on the achievement of formal splendor and scientific rigidity prevented him from succumbing to any kind of sentimental or emotional immediacy.

With the exception of the sonnets included in the section entitled, "Nature and Dreams," Heredia's *Trophées* reveal the skilful transposition of such basically emotional themes as love, death, and the fugacity of time from a personal to an essentially aesthetic level. The discernible lyrical tension in the sonnets stems precisely from the attempt to control the purely emotional responses in order to achieve the desired aesthetic impact. Like Gautier and Leconte de Lisle before him, Heredia sought to fashion works of durable beauty in his poetry. If the best sonnets succeed in conveying Latin strength, Greek beauty, and Hispanic grandeur, such effects are derived from the poet's painstaking fusion of technique, erudition, and intuition.

Heredia patiently reworked each of his sonnets before he allowed them to be collected for publication as *Les Trophées* in 1893. Much of the credit for the formal excellence of the volume may be attributed to Leconte de Lisle who selflessly and carefully corrected the poems which Heredia insisted on submitting to him for comment and approval.[1] Heredia publicly acknowledged his debt to the official mentor of the Parnassian school in an interview with Jules Huret on the state of poetry in France: "Thanks to our cordial relationship, I have been able to appreciate the excellence of your precepts and your advice, and I have been able to benefit from the beauty of your poetic practice. My greatest glory is that I have had the honor of being your pupil." [2] The author of *Les Trophées* served an apprenticeship that was principally formal or technical; he refrained from subscribing to the actively antireligious philosophy entertained by Leconte de Lisle and his followers. That Heredia was allowed to maintain his curious espousal of Parnassian principle and Catholicism within the group speaks eloquently in behalf of the breadth of views tolerated by poets especially remembered for their rigid observance of the rules of prosody.

As epic poems, *Les Trophées* evolved loosely and unsystematically from individual sonnets written by the poet at different intervals during his career on different periods of history. If a unity may be discerned in the collection, it stems from its obvious preoccupation with historicity which constituted the basis of Heredia's poetics. *Les Trophées* pay tribute to the glorious monuments of the past weaved from man's undying aspiration throughout the ages. The fact of the matter is that *Les Trophées* proceed from no preconceived conception of the poet with respect to the conscious elaboration of an epic in the sense of Lamartine's *Visions* and Hugo's *Légende des siècles*. To a significant extent, the idea of associating Heredia's sonnets with the epic originated from the five divisions into which he grouped the twenty-five sonnets that appeared in the 1876 edition of the *Parnasse contemporain.* The one hundred and eighteen sonnets that comprised *Les Trophées* of 1893 retained the five classifications which lend the collection its historical dimension. *Les Trophées* are the poetical embodiment of Heredia's scholarly appreciation of history and of his personal pilgrimages to Greece, Rome, and the Orient. The sonnets trace man's human evolution from the Antiquity of Greece and Sicily to the Middle Ages and the Renaissance.

"L'Oubli" [Forgetfulness] and "Sur un marbre brisé" [Upon a piece of broken marble], the first and last sonnets of *Les Trophées,* invest the collection with a sense of awe at the acknowledgment of death and universal destruction.[3] Both poems, however, as well as the overwhelming number of sonnets, never disintegrate into purely emotional or sentimental meditations on the transitoriness of existence. The impact which Heredia nearly always succeeds in achieving is aesthetic rather than personal.

Examination of "L'Oubli" reveals the poet's ingenious transfer of personal elements into a more generalized aesthetic appreciation of a given sentiment or emotion. The sonnet form from the sixteenth century remains among the most admirably suited means for tightly controlled composition. Heredia is conscious of its division into two quatrains and two tercets and seeks to endow each section with a unity that is both technical and thematic.

Le temple est en ruine au haut du promontoire.
Et la Mort a mêlé, dans ce fauve terrain,
Les Déesses de marbre et les Héros d'airain
Dont l'herbe solitaire ensevelit la gloire.

Seul, parfois, un bouvier menant ses buffles boire,
De sa conque où soupire un antique refrain
Emplissant le ciel calme et l'horizon marin,
Sur l'azur infini dresse sa forme noire.

La Terre maternelle et douce aux anciens Dieux,
Fait à chaque printemps, vainement éloquente,
Au chapiteau brisé verdir une autre acanthe;

Mais l'Homme indifférent au rêve des aieux
Ecoute sans frémir, du fond des nuits sereines,
La Mer qui se lamente en pleurant les Sirènes.

["The temple is in ruins at the top of the promontory, and in this tawny earth, Death has mingled marble goddesses with bronzed heroes whose fame is buried in the lonely grass. His dark profile against the infinite blue sky, alone, a herdsman leading his buffaloes to drink, at times, fills the calm sky and the blue horizon with the sound of his horn from which there sighs an old refrain. The Earth is gentle and maternal to the ancient gods as each spring, in wasted eloquence, it causes a new acanthus to grow on the broken capital. But man, in his indifference to the aspiration of his ancestors, listens without trembling in the depths of the serene night to the Sea lamenting as she weeps for the Sirens."]

The tone belies nostalgia for a bygone epoch. "L' Oubli" conveys a simplicity which emanates from the condensation of thought and the verbal mastery that are manifest in the sonnet. There is a plastic quality which projects from the design and the color displayed in the quatrains and the tercets. Heredia describes the temple and the herdsman in the two quatrains, then evokes nature in the first tercet in a manner in which it reinforces the temple's description in the first quatrain. The concluding three lines allude to man's indifference and provide the final thrust of the sonnet. Like the Pindaric ode, the sonnet may be compared, structurally, to a kind of miniature dissertation consisting of a thesis, an antithesis, and a synthesis. Like the strophe and the antistrophe of the ode, the two quatrains of the sonnet utilize similar rhythms and rhymes to convey the impression that the two stanzas speak and respond to one another. The tercets assume the function of the synthesis in a dissertation. The last line of the sonnet summarizes the preceding thirteen lines and brings the poem to its close.

Heredia's *chute*, however, differs substantially from

that of his predecessors in the sixteenth century: the final line of the concluding tercet suggests an ascension beyond the formal restrictions and limitations of the sonnet. More often than not, Heredia uses the last line to cast his sonnet into a memorable mold. In the *chute* of "L'Oubli," he insists on nasal sounds to convey the final lament. The nasal sounds produce an echoing or reverberating effect which prolongs indefinitely this nostalgic evocation of Greek antiquity. The sonnet embodies much of what Gautier had sought to accomplish with his so-called "transposition of the arts." Despite the dreamy quality of the last line, the sonnet is literally encrusted in language which possesses a metallic contour. "L'Oubli" conveys a sense of opaqueness which allies it with sculpture and architecture and projects stunning pictorial imagery which identifies it with painting.

Among the poems inserted in the category, "Rome and the Barbarians," "Après Cannes" [After Cannae] is an erudite yet remarkably poetic transposition of the destruction of Cannae during the Second Punic War. Based on Livy's account of the decisive defeat of the Romans by the forces of Hannibal, the sonnet avoids interpreting the historical event from any nineteenth-century perspective. Heredia is content to reconstruct the historical moment artistically; he has no thesis to prove or viewpoint to illustrate. The sonnet evokes a vividly pathetic tableau of a population anxiously awaiting the arrival of the Barbarians in their city. Without straying from Livy's interpretation, Heredia captures the psychology of the collective soul of the people and expresses their fears sympathetically:

Un des consuls tué, l'autre fuit vers Linterne
Ou Venuse. L'Aufide a débordé, trop plein
De morts et d'armes. La foudre au Capitolin
Tombe, le bronze sue et le ciel rouge est terne.

En vain le Grand Pontife a fait un lectisterne
Et consulté deux fois l'oracle sibyllin;

D'un long sanglot l'aïeul, la veuve, l'orphelin
Emplissent Rome en deuil que la terreur consterne.

Et chaque soir la foule allait aux aqueducs,
Plèbe, esclaves, enfants, femmes, vieillards caducs
Et tout ce que vomit Subure et l'ergastule;

Tous anxieux de voir surgir, au dos vermeil
Des Monts Sabins où luit l'oeil sanglant du soleil,
Le chef borgne monté sur l'éléphant Gétule.

["One of the consuls killed, the other flees toward Liternum or to Venusia. The Audifus, filled with dead soldiers and arms, has overflowed. Lightning strikes the capitol, the bronze statues sweat, and the red sky is lustreless. The Pontiff has ordered a feast to the gods in vain, and he has consulted the Sibyl's oracle twice to no avail. The great sobs of the grandfather, the widow, and the orphan fill Rome with mourning and with terrorized consternation. And every evening, the crowd goes to the aqueducts: plebs, slaves, children, women, decrepit old men, and all of those which the slums and the slaves's district emit. All are anxious to see come into view, against the ruby backdrop of the Sabine Hills that are illuminated by the bloodied eye of the sun, the one-eyed leader, seated on the Getulian elephant."]

Heredia's sonnet is replete with astonishingly striking colors which invest the tableau with a stunning and quasi-nightmarish atmosphere that accentuates the desperate plight of the people. The rhythms of the poem communicate a sense of nervous anticipation and of gloom. The overflowing of the first line into the second, *ou Venuse*, translates the state of disarray in Cannae as the surviving consul flees without design to Liternum or Venusia. The enjambement of the third line into the fourth, *tombe*, simulates the frightening sound of crashing thunder and lightning upon the capitol. The truncated effects and the raucous sounds of the eleventh line simulate the rushing of the people to the aqueducts to await their fate. The *chute* or the final line of the sonnet harmonizes perfectly with the title, "Après Cannes": the triumphal arrival of the one-eyed Hannibal suggests continuation of the tableau which has just been described and evoked. The frequent allusions to place names and customs bequeaths the sonnet its stamp of authenticity. Heredia's evocation is rooted in historical fact rather than in his imagination. The poet endows his documentation with a freshness and immediacy through the imaginative handling of formal considerations and factual data.

Heredia's lavish tribute to the heroism and the energy which have motivated the memorable accomplishments of past civilizations bespeaks a pagan if not entirely Lucretian conception of immortality. For all their apparent objectivity, *Les Trophées* betray, at frequent intervals, an almost gnawing preoccupation with the problem of death that risks investing some of the sonnets with an underlying melancholic flavor. Like Gautier before him, Heredia avoided the elaboration of a Romantic cosmogony by asserting that man's thirst for eternity is assuaged through the creation of lasting works of art. In *Les Trophées*, heroic action which contributes to the construction of great civilizations partakes of the permanence of a work of art. The love for glorious deeds and the bold assertion of human life which permeate *Les Trophées* derive directly from the poet's interpretation of the function of art. Heredia associates death with glory; man's energetic effort to realize his goals and ambition serves as ample justification of his existence. The death of the soldier, the conqueror, and of the artist achieves meaning through the dignity of their respective actions which remain as monuments of their respective efforts and achievements. Both, "Le Vieil Orfèvre" [The old goldsmith] and "Sur le Livre des amours de Pierre de Ronsard" ["Concerning the book of the loves of Pierre de Ronsard], from the section entitled, "The Middle Ages and the Renaissance," illustrate Heredia's interpretation of artistic survival. "Le Vieil Orfèvre" unveils the dual plight of Heredia, Christian believer and Parnassian poet, with respect to the thorny question of values and eternity:

> J'ai de plus d'un estoc damasquiné le fer
> Et, pour le vain orgueil de ces oeuvres d'Enfer,
> Aventuré ma part de l'éternelle Vie.
>
> Aussi, voyant mon âge incliner vers le soir,
> Je veux, ainsi que fit Fray Juan de Ségovie,
> Mourir en ciselant dans l'or d'un ostensoir.

["I have exposed more than one rapier's stock, and for the vain pride of these works of Hell, I have gambled away my chances for eternal life. Realizing also that I am growing old and approaching death, like Friar Juan of Segovia, I would like to die while chiseling in the gold of a monstrance."]

In a remarkable reworking of Ronsard's own "Sonnet pour Hélène" [Sonnet for Helen], Heredia's poem on the sixteenth-century French poet commemorates the immortality which he has conferred on the three women he loved through a work of art. Heredia's sonnet cleverly juxtaposes the ephemeral beauty possessed by Marie Dupin, Hélène de Surgères, and Cassandre Salviati to the permanence weaved from the creative imagination and the technical skill of the poet. The two tercets extol the power of the poet:

> Tout meurt. Marie, Hélène et toi, fière Cassandre,
> Vos beaux corps ne seraient qu'une insensible cendre,
> —Les roses et les lys n'ont pas de lendemain—
>
> Si Ronsard, sur la Seine ou sur la blonde Loire,
> N'eût tressé pour vos fronts, d'une immortelle main,
> Aux myrtes de l'Amour le laurier de la Gloire.

["Everything dies. Mary, Helen, and you, haughty Cassandra, your beautiful bodies would be but cold ashes—for roses and lilies do not live to bloom another day—if Ronsard, by the Seine or by the sandy Loire, had not woven for your foreheads, with an immortal hand, the myrtle of love with the laurel of glory."]

"Les Conquérants" is the general title attributed to

a series of eight sonnets originally intended as part of a long epic poem on the Spanish conquerors which Heredia never completed.[4] The first sonnet bearing the title, "Les Conquérants," reconstructs poetically the psychology which motivated the bold undertakings of sea captains and mercenaries in search of gold, adventure, and the unknown. The two quatrains depict the adventurers as they prepare their ship for the voyage to the land of gold. In striking contrast, the two tercets evoke the exotic beauty of the New World which transforms the men from rapacious adventurers to poetic dreamers. The departure of the crew and their brutish lust for gold are splendidly conveyed from the outset by the single image of the fleeing gyrfalcons, large birds of prey. Heredia creates the mood and tone of the sonnet with the first line which centers primarily upon the mental frame of reference of the men who were destined to find immortal glory through their discoveries. The voyage on the ocean is never actually described but only conjured up at night: we witness the men as they hold watch and dream of unknown lands. The *chute* or the last line of "Les Conquérants," unlike the closing line of the traditional sonnet of the sixteenth century, does not summarize the preceding thematic development but rather opens up new poetic perspectives as the conquerors gaze, bewildered and enthralled, at the unknown stars of the new hemisphere.

A sense of grandeur emerges from "Les Conquérants" which is achieved principally by an insistent use of qualifying adjectives which either underscore the urgent aspirations of the men or the prodigious undertaking of the voyage; *hautains, ivres, héroiques, fabuleux, mystérieux, brutal, épiques* are but some of the epithets used to convey the impression of the unusual. The two themes—that of the emotional drive of the conquerors and that of limitless dimensions of dreams—intertwine through the symbols which infuse meaning into the picturesque evocation. Heredia's perfect control and technical mastery have enabled him to suggest the entire epic development of the aspirations of the Span-

ish conquerors within the limited confines of the four-
teen-line sonnet. Every aspect in "Les Conquérants"
aims at forming a single though complex impression of
grandeur. The last word of the poem, *nouvelles*, as much
by its timbre as by its power of evocation, appears to
derive directly from all of the preceding words of the
sonnet:

> *Comme un vol de gerfauts hors du charnier natal,*
> *Fatigués de porter leurs misères hautaines,*
> *De Palos de Moguer, routiers et capitaines*
> *Partaient, ivres d'un rêve héroïque et brutal.*
>
> *Ils allaient conquérir le fabuleux métal*
> *Que Cipango mûrit dans ses mines lointaines,*
> *Et les ventes azilés inclinaient leurs antennes*
> *Aux bords mystérieux du monde Occidental.*
>
> *Chaque soir, espérant des lendemains épiques,*
> *L'azur phosphorescent de la mer des Tropiques*
> *Enchantait leur sommeil d'un mirage doré;*
>
> *Ou, penchés à l'avant des blanches caravelles,*
> *Ils regardaient monter en un ciel ignoré*
> *Du fond de l'Océan des étoiles nouvelles.*

["Like the gyrfalcons fleeing from their native charnel
house, mercenaries and captains, tired of bearing their
miseries with haughtiness, set out from Palos de
Moguer, intoxicated by an heroic and brutal dream.
They were going to conquer the fabulous metal stored
in the far-off mines of Chipangu. The trade winds bent
their antennae in the direction of the mysterious shores
of the western world. Each evening as they anticipated
epic tomorrows, the phosphorescent blue of the tropical
sea enchanted their sleep with golden dreams, or, as
they leaned forward on the decks of their white caravels,
they would watch unknown stars rise from the depths of
the ocean into a strange sky."]

Heredia's fabled impersonalism is perhaps best illustrated in the descriptive tour de force entitled, "Le
Récif de corail" [The coral reef], strategically placed

among the nine sonnets appearing under the rubric,
"The Orient and the Tropics." The sonnet evokes a
dazzling subterranean landscape, bathed in sumptuous
color and counterpointed by the alternating musical
rhythms of silence and sudden movement. The two
quatrains and the first tercet, composed of regular
alexandrines, translate admirably the poet's logically
ordered description of the coral reef without resorting
to any kind of syntactical license. The direct, unen-
cumbered linguistic procedure corresponds perfectly to
the clearly illuminated tableau of the first eleven lines.
Heredia has exercised great care in selecting precisely
those vowels and consonants that render his evocation
both auditorily and visually appealing and arresting.
The landscape basks in resplendently luminous
immobility.

If the two quatrains describe the tableau, the tercets
relate the presence and the ultimate movement of the
fish. The final tercet breaks away from the predictability
of the regular rhythms of the preceding lines to convey
the sudden burst of rapid movement. The enjambement
and the irregular caesura of lines twelve and thirteen
blend with the mobility of the fish. The *chute* suggests
the extinguished energy of the moving fish and a return
to the previous calm by resorting to the regular alexandrine line. The first two lines of the closing tercet
emerge in brief antithesis with the static tableau de-
picted in the rest of the sonnet. In typical fashion,
Heredia restores the colors of the landscape with still
more brilliance in the *chute*. Despite the conspicuous
lack of any idea in the sonnet, "Le Récif de corail,"
Heredia manages to stimulate the reader's imagination
by the manner in which he evokes the images that
dominate his description. Without resorting to emotional intervention, the sonnet succeeds in inducing
reverie.

> *Le soleil sous la mer, mystérieuse aurore,*
> *Eclaire la forêt des coraux abyssins*

Qui mêle, aux profondeurs de ses tièdes bassins,
La bête épanouie et la vivante flore.

Et tout ce que le sel ou l'iode colore,
Mousse, algue chevelue, anémones, oursins,
Couvre de pourpre sombre, en somptueux dessins,
Le fond vermiculé du pâle madrépore.

De sa splendide écaille éteignant les émaux,
Un grand poisson navigue à travers les rameaux;
Dans l'ombre transparente indolemment il rôde;

Et, brusquement, d'un coup de sa nageoire en feu
Il fait, par le cristal morne, immobile et bleu,
Courir un frisson d'or, de nacre et d'émeraude.

["The sun beneath the sea, like the mysterious dawn, illuminates the forest of abyssal coral which mixes, in the depth of its tepid basins, the big animals and the living flora. And all that which the salt of the iodine colors—moss, comose algae, urchins, and anemones—envelops in dark purple and in sumptuous designs the pale stonework of the madrepore. With its magnificent scale, a large fish extinguishes the enamels as it swims through the reeds; it prowls indolently in the transparent shadows. Then, suddenly, with a stroke of its inflamed fin, it causes a golden, nacre and emerald colored shiver to run through the dull blue crystal that remains motionless."]

The twenty-two sonnets comprising the section entitled, "Nature and Dreams," lack the thematic cohesiveness of the four preceding classifications which bequeathed them a temporal unity. The ten poems under the rubric, "The Sea of Brittany," sketch varied impressionistic glimpses of the province's customs and traditions which Heredia links psychologically to the seascape that plays such an important role in the lives of the inhabitants. The sonnets which presumably refer to "Dreams" depart both thematically and technically from the tight format that characterizes most of the *Trophées*. The injection of personal elements into such sonnets as "Le Lit" [The bed] and "Plus Ultra" [More beyond] strays from the apparent rigid impersonalism of the overwhelming number of sonnets in the collection. Yet, the poems possess a remarkable effectiveness in their own right.

"Maris stella" [Star of the sea] evokes with striking vividness the anguish of Breton women who implore the protective vigilance of the Virgin over the seafaring husbands and sons at sea. Heredia achieves once again a balanced contrast between the two quatrains and the two tercets; the former evoke the violent foaming of an angry ocean, while the latter six lines invoke the peace of a more serene countryside. Like most of the twenty-two sonnets which comprise the cycle, "Nature and Dreams," "Maris stella" reveals a distinct preference for themes and attitudes that approach modern times. From a technical viewpoint, the evocation of a contrastive anguish and hope associated with the plight of the Breton women is achieved with considerably less the amount of the usual Parnassian objectivity of the sonnets dealing with subjects more removed in time. "Maris stella" juxtaposes the two sentiments within the framework of a secular and religious context.

The two quatrains bespeak the fear and anxiety of the women as they confront an angry, stormy sea upon which their husbands and sons have set sail. The tercets portray, in sharp contrast, a quasi-ethereal or religious calm: the Angelus, representing spiritual hope, tolls and inspires the women in their bewilderment to invoke the plaintive hymn to the Virgin, protectoress of seamen. Rather than answer or complement one another, the quatrains emerge in sharp antithesis, thematically, to the tercets. The calm alluded to in the last six lines produces a somewhat jarring effect when taken into account with the preceding quatrains. This does not mean that Heredia has failed to approximate the psychology of the Breton women in the sonnet. His association of the material with the spiritual world is achieved, rather, on a more intuitive than purely realistic level.

For all of the precision which he lavishes on the mannerisms and provincial costumes of the women in the first eight lines, the remainder of the poem slips into discernibly vaguer imagery and language. The religious mood that overtakes "Maris stella" proceeds from Heredia's own subjective understanding of a situation which he portrays with something less than his customary meticulousness. The *chute* of "Maris stella" displays once again the poet's remarkable talent for creating effective conclusions. The sonnet ends appropriately with a description of the progressive decrescendo of the tolling bell into a silence that conveys fervent expectancy.

> *Sous les coiffes de lin, toutes, croisant leurs bras*
> *Vêtus de laine rude ou de mince percale,*
> *Les femmes à genoux sur le roc de la cale,*
> *Regardent l'Océan blanchir l'île de Batz.*
>
> *Les hommes, pères, fils, maris, amants, là-bas,*
> *Avec ceux de Paimpol, d'Audierne et de Cancale,*
> *Vers le nord, sont partis pour la lointaine escale.*
> *Que de hardis pêcheurs qui ne reviendront pas!*
>
> *Par dessus la rumeur de la mer et des côtes*
> *Le chant plaintif s'élève, invoquant à voix hautes*
> *L'étoile sainte, espoir des marins en péril;*
>
> *Et l'Angélus, courbant tous ces fronts noirs de hâle,*
> *Des clochers de Roscoff à ceux de Sybiril*
> *S'envole, tinte et meurt dans le ciel rose et pâle.*

["Under the linen coifs, with their arms crossed on their breasts, and dressed in coarse woolens or in thin cotton cambrics, all the women kneel on the rocky dock and watch the ocean's white foams cover the island of Batz. Their men: fathers, husbands, and fiancés went there with those of Paimpol, Audierne, and Cancale to sail northward to some far-off port. These brave fishermen shall not return! Above the noise of the sea and of its shores, the plaintive hymn, invoking the holy star of the sea, the last hope of sailors in distress, rises in loud shrill voices. With all of these sunburnt foreheads bowed, the Angelus from the steeples of Roscoff to those of Sybiril rings, tolls and dies in the pale pink sky."]

No less than four of the last eight sonnets of *Les Trophées* concern themselves explicitly with the problem of death and the conception of human glory. As such, "La Mort de l'aigle" [The eagle's death], "Plus Ultra" [More beyond], "La Vie des morts" [The life of the dead], and "Sur un Marbre brisé" [Upon the broken marble] contribute to the epic intention of the collection. Despite the religious fervor detectable in such poems as "Maris stella" and other sonnets in the Breton cycle, the interpretation advanced by Heredia in these poems underscores a purely pagan or Parnassian conception of permanence. "La Vie des morts" betrays a Lucretian view of death and immortality of matter. The latter idea introduced itself logically and effortlessly into the cult of beauty advocated by the supporters of Art for Art's Sake. Heredia's conception of eternity, in *Les Trophées* at least, is more frequently preoccupied with finding an aesthetic solution to the enigma of human destiny. The glory achieved by man's effort in human endeavor is equated with art.

What bequeaths *Les Trophées* its essentially epic flavor is the inventoried list of accomplishments which betray man's aspiration toward perfection and eternity. Heredia resolves the dilemma of man's aspiration for life and the inevitable fact of death in the last tercet of "La Vie des morts": "Cependant que sacrant le poète et l'ami,/La Gloire nous fera vivre à jamais parmi/Les Ombres que la Lyre a faites fraternelles." ["However as the flames consecrate friend and poet, fame will enable us to live eternally among the shadows which the lyre has rendered bearable."]

Despite a return by the French Parnassian poets to the kind of rigorous formal discipline which succeeded in tempering classical and neoclassical expression during

the seventeenth and eighteenth centuries, poets such as
Heredia differed significantly in mood and in temper
from the defenders of values and traditions established
and accepted during the era of Malherbe and Boileau.
What the Parnassians inherited specifically from classicism was its attitude toward language which sought a
ready identification with the objective or externalized
world of fact. Heredia considered the sonnet a mold
sufficiently exacting to contain and direct his lyricism
within the prescribed limits of such an identifiable
world. His scrupulous concern for erudition and precision was posited on a philosophy which advocated the
possibility of externalizing personal inner experiences
in language that could be readily understood and appreciated.

The so-called neoclassical predisposition of Parnassianism was rooted solely in formal linguistic considerations; the leading poets of the movement exhibited a philosophical frame of reference which was
manifestly linked to post-revolutionary modernism.
Poets such as Gautier, Banville, Leconte de Lisle, and
Heredia displayed increasing awareness to the problems
that beset man in a world bereft of any appreciable
number of universal values or traditions. The Parnassians subscribed to an interpretation of the human
condition which was more existentially and modernly
conceived than the essential definition of human aspirations and values advanced by the practitioners of
French classicism. This curious blend of classical formal
restraint and modern existential anguish is no better
expressed than in Heredia's sonnet, "La Mort de l'aigle,"
inserted in the last section of *Les Trophées*:

> *Quand l'aigle a dépassé les neiges éternelles,*
> *À sa vaste envergure il veut chercher plus d'air*
> *Et le soleil plus proche en un azur plus clair*
> *Pour échauffer l'éclat de ses mornes prunelles.*
>
> *Il s'enlève. Il aspire un torrent d'étincelles.*
> *Toujours plus haut, enflant son vol tranquille et fier,*

Il monte vers l'orage où l'attire l'éclair;
Mais la foudre d'un coup a rompu ses deux ailes.

Avec un cri sinistre, il tournoie, emporté
Par la trombe, et, crispé, buvant d'un trait sublime
La flamme éparse, il plonge au fulgurant abîme.

Heureux qui pour la Gloire ou pour la Liberté,
Dans l'orgueil de la force et l'ivresse du rêve,
Meurt ainsi d'une mort éblouissante et brêve!

["The eagle traveled beyond the eternal snows because
he seeks more air for the vast spread of his wings and a
warmer sun in a clearer sky to restore the brilliance of
his tired eyes. He takes flight. He inhales a torrent of
sparks. Always rising higher and swelling his becalmed,
proud flight, he climbs toward the storm which beckons
him with its lightning. But in a single stroke, a crash
of thunder has broken both his wings. With a baleful
cry, he spins about uncontrollably, carried away by the
whirlwind, and, contorted, he drinks in one last draught
of the scattered wind, and plunges into the flashing
abyss. Happy is he who for fame or for freedom, in the
fulness of strength and during the intoxication of the
dream, dies, thus, such a dazzling and quick death!"]

"La Mort de l'aigle" illustrates the remarkable finesse
and unusual rhetorical control with which Heredia has
managed to externalize urgently felt personal attitudes
in sonnets which possess a subtle yet undeniably lyrical
quality. The poet's craftsmanship is nothing less than
admirable: every word and expression is carefully se-
lected for its contribution to the final effect which
Heredia wishes to fix in his reader's mind. With most
of the sonnets of *Les Trophées*, "La Mort de l'aigle"
remains a model of skilful condensation of a theme
which has inspired other poets to treat with more
passion and in considerably greater length. If Heredia's
meticulous concern for formal precision and technical
mastery allies *Les Trophées* with the spirit of neo-

classical strophic lyricism, his powerful and complex evocation of the great moments of history situates his poetry in the burgeoning tradition of modernism in the nineteenth century. Whatever the personal re-action *Les Trophées* may elicit from the modern reader, Heredia's virtuosity with the sonnet remains unchallengeable.

Notes

1 — From Art for Art's Sake to Parnassianism

1, Albert Cassagne, *La Théorie de l'art pour l'art en France chez les derniers romantiques et les premiers réalistes* (Paris; Lucien Dorbon, 1905), pp. 21–24.

2. Charles de Rémusat in the 12 March 1825 issue of *Le Globe*.

3. Madame de Staël, *De l'Allemagne* (n.p. [London], 1813), vol. 2, p. 6.

4. Ibid., vol. 3, p. 9.

5. Although Quatremère de Quincy published his *Essais sur l'idéal* in 1836, his theories on the autonomy of literature were known as early as 1805 because of his open debates with Emeric David, the defender of the traditional realist aesthetic.

6. *Du Vrai, du beau et du bien*, Essay 7 in the 1836 edition. It is interesting to compare this edition with the subsequent versions of 1846 and 1858, for example, where certain moral restrictions are inserted. These are likely accounted by the fact that Victor Cousin was appointed Minister of Public Education in 1840 and came under heavy attack by the clergy.

7. Théodore Jouffroy, *Cours d'esthétique* (1826), Essay 4. The *Cours d'esthétique* is essentially a revision of Jouffroy's lectures at the Ecole Normale. Sainte-Beuve attended these lectures. See Cassagne, *La Théorie de l'art pour l'art*, p. 41.

8. There were actually four different prefaces written for the *Odes et ballades*: 1822, 1824, 1826 and 1828. My quotation is from the preface of 1826.

9. See "Adresse aux artistes" in the November–December 1831 issue of *La Revue encyclopédique*. The journal had been founded only the previous September.

10. Théophile Gautier, *Préface à Albertus*, 1832.

11. Ibid.

12. See Louise B. Dillingham, *The Creative Imagination of Théophile Gautier* (Bryn Mawr, Pa.: Bryn Mawr College, 1927), pp. 25–26. Gautier gradually drew back from his closest friendly associations and confined his affections in so far as possible to the least exacting objects: his family and his animals.

13. Théophile Gautier, *Mademoiselle de Maupin* (Paris: Garnier, 1966), p. 231.

14. See my study, *Nineteenth-Century French Romantic Poets* (Carbondale: Southern Illinois University Press, 1969), pp. 81–82 for a fuller discussion of the problem.

15. "L'Art" was first published in *L'Artiste* on 13 September 1857 under the title, "A M. Théodore de Banville, réponse à son odelette."

16. Théophile Gautier, *Histoire du Romantisme* (Paris: Charpentier, 1884), p. 216.

17. Théophile Gautier, "Salon de 1837" in the 24 March 1837 issue of *La Presse*.

18. Félicité de Lamennais, *Esquisse d'une philosophie*, ed. Chesnaie (n.p. [Paris], 1841), vol. 8, pp. iii, 133–34.

19. Charles Baudelaire, "Pierre Dupont" in *L'Art romantique* (Paris: Garnier, 1962), p. 556.

20. Ibid., pp. 659–86. Especially: "La poésie, pour peu qu'on veuille descendre en soi-même, interroger son âme, rappeler ses souvenirs d'enthousiasme, n'a pas d'autre but qu'Elle-même."

21. See Edmond Lepelletier, *Paul Verlaine: sa vie, son oeuvre* (Paris: Mercure de France, 1907), pp. 188–89. Paul Souriau, in *Histoire du Parnasse* (Paris: Spes, 1929), p. 251, suggests that Mendès and Ricard sought to diminish Leconte de Lisle's influence by ignoring his objection to the title of the collection.

22. The following fourteen poets published in each of the three issues of the *Parnasse contemporain*: Banville, Cazalis, Coppée, Dierx, des Essarts, Heredia, Leconte de Lisle, André Lemoyne, Catulle Mendès, Mérat, Xavier de Ricard, Antoine Renaud, Sully Prudhomme, and Valade. The *Parnasse contemporain* attracted the attention of other poets not usually associated with the movement. Rimbaud, for example, read the Parnassian journal assiduously and hoped

to have such poems as "Credo in unam" and "Sensation" published in the 1871 issue. He wrote to Théodore de Banville in this respect but was informed that he applied too late for inclusion. See Wallace Fowlie, *Rimbaud: A Critical Study* (Chicago; University of Chicago Press, 1965), pp. 10–13.

23. Interview published by Jules Huret in *Enquête sur l'évolution littéraire* (Paris: Charpentier, 1891), pp. 288–89.

24. The prefaces to the *Poèmes antiques*, the *Poèmes barbares* and the *Poèmes tragiques* have been grouped and are published together in the posthumous volume that includes the *Derniers poèmes* in 1894.

25. Gustave Flaubert, *Correspondance*, vol. 2 (Paris: Charpentier, 1899), pp. 199–200.

26. Jules Lemaître, *Les Contemporains*, vol. 2 (Paris: Lecène et Oudin, 1885), p. 45.

27. See Cassagne, *La Théorie de l'art pour l'art*, pp. 267–68 for a fuller treatment of the question.

2 – Théophile Gautier and the Quest for Objectivity

1. For a lucid exposition of Gautier's earlier poetry, see Chapters One and Two of Louise B. Dillingham, *The Creative Imagination of Théophile Gautier* (Bryn Mawr, Pa.: Bryn Mawr College, 1927).

2. Gabriel Brunet, "Théophile Gautier, poète." *Mercure de France*, 15 October 1922, pp. 289–332.

3. P. E. Charvet, *A Literary History of France, Vol. 4, The Nineteenth Century* (New York: Barnes and Noble, 1967), p. 308.

4. See Albert Thibaudet, *Histoire de la Littérature française de 1789 à nos jours* (Paris: Stock, 1936), p. 184: "Le peintre manque de musique et d'au-delà. Ce cercle d'idées limité aux lettres, à l'art, au noir sur le blanc, à la ligne et à la couleur, ne va pas sans automatisme, sans monotonie, sans tout-fait et sans prévu." For André Gide's comment, see Pierre-Georges Castex, *Le Conte fantastique en France de Nodier à Maupassant.* (Paris: Corti, 1951), p. 214. Castex quotes Gide with regard to Gautier: ". . . sa cécité pour tout ce qui n'est pas le monde extérieur."

5. Gustave Lanson, *Histoire de la Littérature française* (Paris; Hachette, 1951), p. 196.

6. Théophile Gautier, *Mademoiselle de Maupin* (Paris: Garnier, 1966), p. 243.

7. See Dillingham's *The Creative Imagination of Théophile Gautier*, pp. 75–77 for a perceptive account of the idea of concealment and revelation of beauty in Gautier's narrative fiction.

8. Albert B. Smith, *Ideal and Reality in the Fictional Narratives of Théophile Gautier* (Gainesville: University of Florida Press, 1969), pp. 1–64. Smith analyzes Gautier's evolving notion of the character of the ideal in the sixteen narratives that he published between 1831 and 1865. This monograph elucidates the whole question of the narrative in Gautier and indirectly illumines the author's poetic code.

9. Théophile Gautier, *Spirite* (Paris: Charpentier, 1886), pp. 110–11.

10. For a detailed account of the manner in which Gautier undertook the reworking of the various poems in *Emaux et camées*, see Spoelberch de Lovenjoul's informative study, *Histoire des oeuvres de Théophile Gautier*, 2 vols. (Paris: Charpentier, 1887).

11. Among the critics of the nineteenth century who denied the existence of ideas in Gautier's poetry were Scherer, Faguet, and Brunetière. Sainte-Beuve, on the contrary, defended Gautier with eloquence in *Nouveaux Lundis*, vol. 6 (Paris: Calmann-Lévy, 1862), p. 289.

12. Pierre Michel, *La Poésie parnassienne* (Paris: Foucher, n.d.), pp. 15–18.

13. B. L. Nicholas in *French Literature and Its Background: The Late Nineteenth Century*, ed. John Cruickshank (Oxford: Oxford University Press, 1969), p. 23.

14. A. E. Carter, *The Idea of Decadence in French Literature: 1830–1900* (Toronto: University of Toronto Press, 1958), pp. 6–7.

15. Théophile Gautier, *Mademoiselle de Maupin*, p. 315.

16. Georges Poulet, *Studies in Human Time* (New York: Harper & Brothers, Publishers, Harper Torchbooks, 1956), p. 248.

17. Joris-Karl Huysmans, *Against Nature*, trans. Robert Baldick (Baltimore: Penguin Books, 1959), p. 189.

3 – Théodore de Banville and the Obsession With Formal Perfection

1. John Charpentier, *Théodore de Banville: l'homme et son oeuvre* (Paris: Perrin, 1925), p. 109.

2. Maurice Souriau, *Histoire du Parnasse* (Paris: Spes, 1929), pp. 62–67.

3. Ibid., p. 65.

4. Anatole France, *La Vie littéraire*, vol. 4 (Paris: Calmann-Lévy, 1889), p. 236.

5. René Lalou, *Histoire de la Littérature contemporaine* (Paris: Crès, 1922), p. 8.

6. Fernand Calmettes, *Leconte de Lisle et ses amis* (Paris: Motteroz, n.d.), p. 26.

4 – Leconte de Lisle and the Historical Imagination

1. See Richard Chadbourne, "The Generation of 1848: Four Writers and their Affinities," *Essays in French Literature* 5 (1968): 1–21, for a stimulating discussion of Leconte de Lisle's mental affinity with Renan, Baudelaire, and Flaubert.

2. Irving Putter, *The Pessimism of Leconte de Lisle: Sources and Evolution* (Berkeley and Los Angeles: University of California Press, 1954), p. 37. Especially: "Not only does he already find the present wanting with respect to the past, but he is persuaded that the future too will be dark."

3. In his essay on Lamartine, de Lisle stated: "A real poet never allows himself to become the systematic or involuntary echo of the public mind. It is for other men to learn to feel and think like him."

4. Chadbourne, "The Generation of 1848," p. 8.

5. Jean Psichari, *Autour de la Grèce* (Paris: Calmann-Lévy, 1897), pp. 165–70.

6. See Putter, *The Pessimism of Leconte de Lisle*, pp. 4–6 and Alison Fairlie, *Leconte de Lisle's Poems on the Barbaric Races* (Cambridge: At the University Press, 1947), chapters 1–4.

7. Paul Souriau, *Histoire du Parnasse* (Paris: Spes, 1929), p. 181.

8. In this connection, see Gladys Falshaw, *Leconte de Lisle et l'Inde* (Paris: D'Arthez, 1923), pp. 191–96. Professor

Falshaw suggests that Leconte de Lisle mixes Brahmanism with Buddhism in such poems as "Bhagavat" and "La Vision de Brahma."

9. Leconte de Lisle, *Histoire populaire du Christianisme* (Paris: Alphonse Lemerre, 1871), p. 140.

10. Ibid.

11. Charles-Augustin de Sainte-Beuve, *Causeries du Lundi*, vol. 5 (Paris: Garnier, n.d.), p. 314.

12. Putter, *The Pessimism of Leconte de Lisle*, pp. 233–35.

13. The initial edition of the *Poèmes barbares* contained thirty-six poems, most of which had appeared singly in such journals as the *Revue des deux mondes*, the *Revue contemporaine* and the *Revue Européenne*. The 1872 edition was increased to seventy-two poems and the final edition of 1878 contained seventy-seven poems.

14. Anatole France, *La Vie littéraire*, vol. 1 (Paris: Calmann-Lévy, 1889), p. 96.

15. Joseph Vianey, *Les Sources de Leconte de Lisle* (Montpellier: Coulet, 1907), pp. 136–39.

16. Charles Baudelaire, "Leconte de Lisle" in *L'Art romantique* (Paris: Garnier, 1962), p. 781.

17. See Gérard de Nerval, *Voyage en orient*, vol. 2 (Paris: Garnier, 1966), pp. 632–33. Adoniram, who possesses the Promethean spirit, learns from Tubal-Cain, blacksmith for the master builder, that he derives from the descendants of Cain who escaped the Flood by taking refuge underground.

18. Anatole France, *La Vie littéraire*, vol. 1, p. 104.

5—José-Maria de Heredia and the Poetics of Historicity

1. See Mauriace Souriau, *Histoire du Parnasse* (Paris: Spes, 1929), pp. 292–95, for a fuller account of de Lisle's influence on Heredia.

2. Jules Huret, *Enquête sur l'évolution littéraire* (Paris: Charpentier, 1891), pp. 310–11.

3. Emile Moussat, *Les Sonnets de José-Maria de Heredia* (Paris: Foucher, n.d.), p. 39. Heredia divided his sonnets into the categories: 1: Greece and Sicily; 2: Rome and the Barbarians; 3: The Middle Ages and the Renaissance; 4: The Orient and the Tropics; 5: Nature and Dreams. "L'Oubli"

appeared under the first classification and "Sur un marbre brisé" was included in the last division.

4. Heredia read widely in the works of Bernal Diaz del Castillo, W. H. Prescott, and Washington Irving in preparation for an epic he wished to entitle, *La Détresse d'Atahuallpa.*

Selected Bibliography

Anthologies

Boase, Alan M. *The Poetry of France: 1800–1900*. Vol. 3. London: Methuen and Company, 1967.

Galland, Joseph and Roger Cros. *Nineteenth-Century French Verse*. New York: Appleton-Century-Crofts, 1959.

Grant, Elliott M. *French Poetry of the Nineteenth Century*. Second Edition. New York: Macmillan Co., 1962.

Hartley, Anthony. *The Penguin Book of French Verse: The Nineteenth Century*. Baltimore: Penguin Books, 1963.

Parmée, Douglas. *Twelve French Poets*. New York: David McKay, 1962.

Schinz, Albert. *Nineteenth-Century French Readings*. Vol. 2. New York: Henry Holt, 1955.

General Studies on Parnassianism

Bays, Gwendolyn. *The Orphic Vision: Seer Poets from Novalis to Rimbaud*. Lincoln: University of Nebraska Press, 1964.

Bornecque, J.-H. and P. Cogny. *Réalisme et Naturalisme*. Paris: Hachette, 1958.

Brereton, Geoffrey. *An Introduction to the French Poets: Villon to the Present Day*. New York: Barnes and Noble, 1960.

Canat, René. *Du Sentiment de la solitude morale chez les Romantiques et les Parnassiens*. Geneva: Slatkine Reprints, 1967.

Carter, A. E. *The Idea of Decadence in French Literature: 1830–1900*. Toronto: University of Toronto Press, 1958.

———. *Verlaine: A Study in Parallels*. Toronto: University of Toronto Press, 1969.

Cassagne, Albert. *La Théorie de l'art pour l'art en France*

chez les derniers romantiques et les premiers réalistes.
Paris: Lucien Dorbon, n.d.

Chadbourne, Richard M. "The Generation of 1848: Four
Writers and Their Affinities." *Essays in French Literature*
5 (1968): 1–21.

Charvet, P. E. *A Literary History of France: The Nineteenth
Century 1789–1870.* New York: Barnes and Noble, 1967.

Cruickshank, John, ed. *French Literature and Its Background.* Vol. 5, *The Late Nineteenth Century.* Oxford:
Oxford University Press, 1969.

Dumesnil, René. *Le Réalisme et le Naturalisme.* Paris: Del
Duca – De Gigord, 1955.

Fowlie, Wallace. *Rimbaud: A Critical Study.* Chicago: University of Chicago Press, 1965.

Gallois, Daniel and J.-B. Piéri. *Le XIXe Siècle.* Paris:
Eugène Belin, 1960.

Michel, Pierre. *La Poésie parnassienne.* Paris: Foucher, n.d.

Martino, Pierre. *Parnasse et Symbolisme.* Paris: Armand
Colin, 1954.

Peyre, Henri. *Louis Ménard (1822–1901).* New Haven: Yale
University Press, 1932.

Pouilliart, Raymond. *Le Romantisme III: 1869–1896.* Paris:
Arthaud, 1968.

Poulet, Georges. *Studies in Human Time.* New York: Harper & Brothers, Publishers, Harper Torchbooks, 1956.

Salomon, Pierre. *Précis d'Histoire de la littérature française.*
New York: St. Martin's Press, 1964.

Souriau, Maurice. *Histoire du Parnasse.* Paris: Spes, 1929.

Thibaudet, Albert. *Histoire de la littérature française de
1789 à nos jours.* Paris: Stock, 1936.

On Gautier

Brunet, Gabriel. "Théophile Gautier, poète." *Mercure de
France,* 15 October 1922, pp. 289–332.

Delvaille, Bernard. *Théophile Gautier.* Paris: Pierre Seghers,
1968.

Dillingham, Louise B. *The Creative Imagination of Théophile Gautier: A Study in Literary Psychology.* Bryn Mawr,
Pa.: Bryn Mawr College, 1927.

Gautier, Théophile. *Poésies diverses.* Edited by Ferdinand
Gohin and Roger Tisserand. Paris: Larousse, 1929.

————. *Emaux et camées*. Edited by Jean Pommier and Georges Matoré. Geneva: Droz, 1947.

Giraud, Raymond. "Gautier's Dehumanization of Art." *L'Esprit Créateur* 3 (1963): 3–8.

Smith, Albert B. *Ideal and Reality in the Fictional Narratives of Théophile Gautier*. Gainesville: University of Florida Press, 1969.

Spoelberch de Louvenjoul. *Histoire des oeuvres de Théophile Gautier*. 2 vols. Paris: Charpentier, 1887.

On Banville

Banville, Théodore de. *Oeuvres*. 3 vols. Paris: Alphonse Lemerre, 1925.

Charpentier, John. *Théodore de Banville: l'homme et son oeuvre*. Paris: Perrin, 1925.

On de Lisle

Calmettes, Fernand. *Leconte de Lisle et ses amis*. Paris: Motteroz, n.d.

de Lisle, Leconte. *Poésies complètes*. 4 vols. Paris: Alphonse Lemerre, 1927–28.

————. *Poèmes choisis*. Edited by Edmond Eggli. Manchester: The University Press, 1959.

Estève, Edmond. *Leconte de Lisle: l'homme et l'oeuvre*. Paris: Boivin, 1922.

Fairlie, Alison. *Leconte de Lisle's Poems on the Barbarian Races*. Cambridge: At the University Press, 1947.

Falshaw, Gladys. *Leconte de Lisle et l'Inde*. Paris: D'Arthez, 1923.

Flottes, Pierre. *Leconte de Lisle*. Paris: Boivin-Hatier, 1954.

Jobit, Pierre. *Leconte de Lisle et le mirage de l'île natale*. Paris: De Boccard, 1951.

Moreau, Pierre. "A propos du centenaire des *Poèmes barbares*." *Symposium* 18 (1964): 197–214.

Priou, Jules-Marie. *Leconte de Lisle*. Paris: Pierre Seghers, 1966.

Putter, Irving. *The Pessimism of Leconte de Lisle: Sources and Evolution*. Berkeley and Los Angeles: University of California Press, 1954.

————. *The Pessimism of Leconte de Lisle: The Work and*

the Time. Berkeley and Los Angeles: University of California Press, 1961.

————. *Lettres inédites à Emilie Leforestier: La dernière illusion de Leconte de Lisle*. Berkeley and Los Angeles: University of California Press, 1968.

Vianey, Joseph. *Les Poèmes barbares de Leconte de Lisle*. Paris: Nizet, n.d.

Whiteley, J. H. *Etude sur la langue et le style de Leconte de Lisle*. Oxford: Oxford University Press, 1910.

On Heredia

Heredia, José-Maria de. *Les Trophées*. Paris: Alphonse Lemerre, 1895.

Ibrovac, Miodrag. *José-Maria de Heredia*. 2 vols. Paris: Les Presses françaises, 1929.

Moussat Emile. *Les Sonnets de José-Maria de Heredia*. Paris: Foucher, n.d.

Index